The Birdk
Guide
AMAZONS

The Birdkeepers' Guide
AMAZONS

GREG GLENDELL

T.F.H. Publications, Inc.

Published by
T.F.H. Publications, Inc.
One TFH Plaza
Third and Union Avenues
Neptune City, NJ 07753

Copyright © 2007 by Interpet Publishing, Ltd.
All rights reserved

ISBN 978-0-7938-0653-9

Printed and Bound in China
05 06 07 08 09 1 3 5 7 9 8 6 4 2

Library of Congress Cataloging-in-Publication
Data
Glendell, Greg.
  Birdkeepers' guide to Amazons / Greg Glendell.
    p. cm.
  Includes index.
  ISBN 978-0-7938-0653-9 (alk. paper)
  1. Amazon parrots. I. Title.
SF473.P3G55 2008
636.6'865—dc22
                    2007035807

This book has been published with the
intent to provide accurate and authoritative
information in regard to the subject matter
within. While every reasonable precaution
has been taken in preparation of this book,
the author and publisher expressly disclaim
responsibility for any errors, omissions, or
adverse effects arising from the use or
application of the information
contained herein. The techniques
and suggestions are used at the
reader's discretion and are not to
be considered a substitute for
veterinary care. If you suspect a
medical problem, consult your
veterinarian.

The Leader In Responsible Animal Care
For Over 50 Years!®
www.tfh.com
CENTRAL
Garden & Pet

Greg Glendell, BSc (Hons)
Greg Glendell has had a
lifelong interest in birds. As
an amateur ornithologist he
has carried out fieldwork on
bird habitat requirements and
the breeding biology of native
British birds. Following his degree
in Environmental Science, which
included coursework on animal and
human behavior, he worked in wildlife
conservation. He acquired his first parrot,
a blue-fronted Amazon, in 1986 and this led to
him developing a deep interest in these birds. He has bred
parrots but no longer does so as
there is a surplus of these birds in
need of good homes. He keeps
several parrots including African
greys, Amazons, and a Meyer's.
Greg works as the UK's only full-
time pet parrot behavioral
consultant and is based in
Somerset. You can e-mail Greg at
mail@greg-parrots.co.uk and visit his
website: www.greg-parrots.co.uk
<http://www.greg-parrots.co.uk/>
for more details of his
consultancy. He is the author
of *Breaking Bad Habits in
Parrots* (2007).

Acknowledgements
Greg would like to thank
Rachel Lewis for her
comments on the text. Bertie
and Martha performed to
their usual high standards.

CONTENTS

CHAPTER 1

Introducing Amazon parrots

There are dozens of different species of Amazon parrots. Most are medium-sized to fairly large birds. While most Amazons kept as pets are bred in captivity, all 'Amazon' parrots come originally from Central or South America. They are well-known as pet birds and many of them will imitate human speech, though not with the clarity of voice heard in grey parrots.

Loud, extrovert birds

This book explores the range of species of Amazon parrots, concentrating on those types often seen as pet or companion birds. Details of all aspects of the care of companion Amazons is covered, including housing in cages and aviaries, recommended diets, basic training including the teaching of flight requests, how to overcome any behavioral problems, and aspects of health and first aid. There is also a section on how to recover a lost Amazon, in case you lose your bird. While most Amazons share many similar characteristics as companion birds, there are important differences between some species and the details of these are included as well.

Amazon parrots are not usually quiet or shy birds. Once they are used to their home, most reveal their extrovert nature. They can be very loud and demanding birds to keep. With proper care, particularly appropriate training, and by teaching your bird to accept some simple requests, you should have a parrot who is a joy to be with. But Amazon parrots are not quiet in any sense of the word. They are full of character, and playful—even boisterous—birds whose proper care requires the bird's keeper to have a sound knowledge of their bird's true needs.

A yellow-naped Amazon. Like most Amazons, these are essentially green birds. This is one of the larger species; about the size of a crow.

⇧ **Once used to their carers,** Amazons are often extrovert birds. Unlike some other parrots, many are also quite confident in the company of strangers.

Basic training, as detailed ⇨
later in this book, is the key
to developing a good
relationship with
your bird.

Reward-based
training works well
with Amazons.

⇦ **Amazons are long-lived birds**
with a similar lifespan to humans,
around 50 to 70 years. The bond
between the bird and its carer can be
complex and last for many decades.

Most Amazons have loud ⇨
voices as part of their normal
vocal repertoire. Adult
birds also indulge in
regular screaming
sessions, usually in the
mornings and evenings,
for 20 minutes or so.

The origin of Amazon parrots

There are at least 31 species of Amazon parrots belonging to the *Amazona* genus of parrots. While Amazon parrots are a large group, less than a dozen species are commonly kept as pet or companion birds.

While all Amazon parrots originate from South and Central American countries, they are certainly not confined to the Amazon region from which they derive their name. Species can be found as far south as southern Argentina to Mexico in the north and on many of the Caribbean islands. As a group of birds, parrots have been around for over 35 million years and during this time, Amazon parrots have evolved into a varied range of species, but they are all dependent on life in the trees for most of their needs. Trees provide the food consisting of fruits, nuts and seeds, as well as nesting holes for breeding.

Stocky, short-tailed green birds

Amazon parrots range in size from the small white-fronted or spectacled Amazon (10in/25cm long) to the very large imperial Amazon which is as big as a crow at 18in (48cm) long. Most species are pigeon-sized birds and are quite stocky, with short, square tails, and the plumage is predominantly leaf-green. At first glance many of the species look very similar to one another. However, each has distinct patches of red, yellow, blue, or orange on the wings, tail, and head. The colors on the head are particularly helpful in telling the species apart.

As with other parrots, Amazons have powerful hooked beaks that are used to process their food and as a third "hand" when climbing around in the trees. While the legs seem quite short, they actually have a long reach and again this aids them while climbing. Like all parrots the feet have four toes; two face forward and two face backwards. The joints in the bird's feet allow them to walk in line along a branch rather than having to side-step along a branch as most other birds have to. The eyes of Amazons are usually a bright orange or red and the birds can control their iris by "flashing" their eyes when excited.

Introducing Amazon parrots

⇦ **Note the long reach** of the apparently short legs. This ability helps them to climb with ease through the trees.

⇧ **Amazons can dilate** and contract their irises at will.

⇦ **Amazons have a waddling** but relatively confident gait.

⇧ **While some smaller parrots** often hop, Amazons always walk or run and rarely hop. They are very nimble birds when climbing around in tree branches.

⇦ **The almost uniform leaf-green colour** of Amazons allows them to remain well camouflaged in their natural habitat. Amazons are never found very far from trees and most species live in tropical forests, such as are illustrated here.

The diversity of Amazon parrots

A mazon parrots, though chiefly looking green when at rest, are in fact one of the most colorful groups of parrots. Their mainly leaf-green color allows them to hide from predators in tree foliage. When at rest, some of their bright colors remain hidden, but when they are in flight, more of the patterns on their wings and tail are revealed. With similar-sized species, these small differences in color, together with differences in their contact calls,

⇧ *Double yellow-headed Amazon.*

allows us to tell them apart. When seen close-up, there are also small but significant differences in head and beak color which further aid identification.

⇧ GREEN-CHEEKED AMAZON

Color This bird is rare in aviculture and is a specially protected species. Mainly plain green with single red patch on wing. Red on forehead with small area of blue behind. Beak is always pale horn-colored.
Size 12in (30cm). A little smaller than the more common orange-winged Amazon.
Voice This bird has a very large repertoire of loud calls: whistles, screams, and harsh rasping and chattering. Not known for its abilities to mimic human speech.
Temperament A rather wary, nervous bird, yet inclined to be very loud. It requires someone who is calm and confident in handling it.

⇦ RED-LORED AMAZON

Color Green with yellow-green tail and red on some wing feathers. The *lores* are the areas between the beak and the eye, hence the bird's name. The legs are gray and the bill color varies from pale horn to dark gray.
Size 12-14in (30-35cm). A medium-sized Amazon similar in size to a pigeon.
Voice A wide range of loud, harsh, often metallic calls and alarm notes. Usually of two or three syllables.
Temperament These birds are quite loud, but usually have a gentle, trusting nature as pet birds.

◁ BLUE-FRONTED AMAZON

Color Variable amounts of blue and yellow on the head. The beak is always very dark or black. Prominent yellow and/or red on bend of wing. Yellow on leg feathers.

Size 14.5in (37cm). Larger and slimmer than the orange-winged Amazon.

Voice Has loud repeated screaming sessions as part of its normal behavior. Usually learns human speech easily; good mimic.

Temperament Very extroverted bold birds. Males can be very aggressive for a few months during each breeding season (spring). But beware, they have very powerful beaks—this species is not suitable for families with young children.

YELLOW-NAPED AMAZON ▷

Color Mainly uniform green with red on bend of the wing and red secondary feathers. The only Amazon with a large yellow patch on the back of its neck. Beak is always dark grey; grey legs and feet.

Size Up to 15in (38cm). This is one of the largest Amazons. Stocky build.

Voice A large range of loud calls; whistles, screeches, and harsher deeper notes as well. Mimics human speech very well.

Temperament Loud and outgoing. Well-trained birds can be good companions, but small children should not handle this species.

◁ ORANGE-WINGED AMAZON

Color Similar to blue-fronted Amazon but the head is squarer. The blue on the head is a powder-blue color, rather than turquoise-blue as in the blue-fronted Amazon and the eyes are larger and usually darker on an orange-winged Amazon. The bend of the wing has some yellow feathers, but never orange as with the blue-fronted.

Size 12.5in (32cm). Slightly smaller than a blue-fronted.

Voice Can be very loud; has loud three-note contact call.

Temperament Very confiding, steady, but rather introverted birds. Much gentler than most Amazons, but some can be very nervous.

CHAPTER 2

Amazon parrots in the wild

Most species of Amazons are highly social birds, living for some or all of their lives within a flock of their own kind. Groups of Amazons may be as small as a family party of four or five birds or as large as a flock of hundreds of birds. In most cases, as they wake up each morning, the birds will get ready to set off in search of food found elsewhere in the forest or in the more open woodland habitat that some species live in. Amazons are generally rather loud birds. Their repertoire is a mixture of whistles, squawks and some loud harsh screeching sounds. Most Amazons have regular screaming sessions, briefly in the early morning, soon after waking up and again in the evening. After waking, they soon leave their roosting site and fly to the first feeding sites which may be many miles away. If you have the chance to see a flock of wild Amazons, you can clearly see that most birds fly as pairs, with the same two birds staying close to one another during flight and when alighting. The birds may feed communally for much of the daytime, often flying considerable distances between feeding sites. Amazons fly at 35 to 45mph (56 to 72kph) so they are able to cover huge areas of habitat within a few minutes' flying time.

A wide range of foods are eaten

Amazons eat a mixture of fruits, nuts, flowers, seeds, and young shoots on a range of forest trees, including some palm trees. When feeding in the trees they use their strong feet, aided by their equally strong beaks as they climb among the branches. They have a range of techniques for dealing with different foods. Seeds and small nuts are easily cracked open with their powerful crushing beak, and larger nuts and fruits can be held in one foot as they use the beak to get at the most nutritious parts. Tender shoots and leaves form part of their diet, and Amazons can easily, climb out to reach these on the tips of the branches. Soft fruit is also eaten, and the birds chew up the fruit pulp with the beak and then drink the resulting juice. Some Amazons come down to the ground occasionally to feed, and several species eat soil at clay-licks in South America. This habit of eating soil is thought to help them to be able to eat other foods which would be toxic in the absence of the soil to neutralize the poisons they sometimes ingest.

⇧ **Like most adult Amazons,** these red-loreds live together as a pair and fly and feed together, usually within a flock.

⇦ **Amazons are sometimes seen as pests** when they eat agricultural crops, such as these yellow-naped Amazons are doing with these bananas.

The red-tailed Amazon is ⇨ primarily a fruit eater. It inhabits coastal regions of eastern Brazil but is now quite rare in the wild.

Flock behavior in the wild

When the feeding flock includes breeding birds, these will travel between the flock and their nesting sites from time to time throughout the day. In the heat of the afternoon the birds have a quiet siesta in the shade of the trees for an hour or two when they doze (*left*) and preen avoiding other activities when it is very hot. In the late afternoon they commence feeding again. After this, they return to their roosting site, occasionally flying while it is almost dark. On most days in the birds' tropical or sub-tropical habitat it rains, and the rain may come down in sudden heavy showers, drenching everything, including the birds. But Amazons are enthusiastic when a good shower is available, and they will roll around in the trees and open their wings to get thoroughly soaked in the rain. These regular showers are vital in keeping their feathers in good condition. After the rain, they spend much time shaking the excess water off, preening, and tidying up their feathers.

Amazons enjoy playful squabbling

Since most Amazons come from tropical areas there is little change in daylight length throughout the year, and the birds get equal amounts (12 hours) of darkness and daylight each day. Amazons can be quite rough when they play with each other, and they may indulge in mock fights and tease each other as they clamber through the trees. They live in a habitat where food is quite plentiful and although they will spend many hours feeding and flying between feeding sites, non-breeding birds have quite a bit of free time to enjoy themselves.

Amazons are adaptable and intelligent birds with a large repertoire of calls and postures which they use as their language. In this way, they inform other members of their flock how they are reacting to things going on around them and what action to take on seeing a predator. Like other parrots, Amazons are vulnerable to predation and this may come from hawks, mammals (including humans), and reptiles. They use their calls to warn each other of the different types of threat they may encounter and the best action to take. The flock may have to make split-second decisions about whether to flee from a hawk or just hide from the danger within the trees as the predator passes by. The birds are highly aware of everything going on around them and they retain this very alert nature as companion birds in our homes.

⇧ *A flock of mealy Amazons* in typical treetop location. Note how some birds perch together as pairs.

⇦ *The birds spend* a lot of time preening and can reach most parts with the beak.

⇦ *Birds within a flock* may take turns to be on guard duty, ready to warn if predators are seen. This mealy Amazon scans the sky warily for hawks.

Nesting and breeding

Like other parrots, Amazons nest in holes in trees. Generally these are existing holes, high up in the trunk of a tree. Often, an existing small hole is enlarged, and Amazons are easily capable of excavating these using their powerful beaks. The birds do not carry any material to the nesting hole; the eggs, usually two to four, are laid on the wood chippings of the floor of the hole. The female takes on most of the responsibility for incubation and caring for the chicks, but males do help as well. The male will return regularly to feed his mate on regurgitated food, which he stores in his crop. This is vital for the female when she is incubating the eggs and brooding the very young chicks.

After 20 to 25 days' incubation, the chicks start to call from within the egg as they begin to establish their contact calls with their parents. The eggs will then hatch two or three days later. The chicks emerge blind but covered with some grey down feathers. The parents feed the chicks on partially digested regurgitated food, and the babies develop quite rapidly. Usually they are ready to take their first flight and leave the nest (to fledge) by 10 to 13 weeks of age. At this age, the young birds are very naïve and clumsy and highly vulnerable to attacks from predators. They are also quite incapable of feeding themselves and will rely on their parents for many weeks or even many months after leaving the nest.

While the urge to fly is very strong in the baby birds at this age, their first few flights may end in crash landings as the skills of flying have to be developed by trial and error. At this age, they are reliant on their parents for a good degree of protection from predators, and it is only over time that they learn to fly well and fast like their parents. Many recently fledged birds fail to survive, but those who learn fast, remain alert at all times, and develop their flying skills rapidly stand a good chance of surviving. The birds spend two to four years with the flock as nonbreeding youngsters. On sexual maturity, they begin to pair up and seek out nesting holes for breeding. By this time, those which have managed to survive will have acquired a great deal of knowledge about their own flock, the vast areas available to them for feeding in, and the best ways of avoiding dangerous predators.

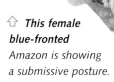

⇧ **This female blue-fronted** Amazon is showing a submissive posture.

⇧ *Amazons are born blind and almost naked.*
A pair of red-lored ⇨
Amazons relax.

⇩ *Male Amazons will **often** regurgitate food from their crop as part of their courtship behavior.*

CHAPTER 3

Amazons as companion birds

Amazons are one of the most popular types of parrots kept as pets, and they can be found throughout the world as companion animals. They tend to be more extroverted birds than some other parrots. In the right hands, they are very lively and outgoing with a keen interest in everything going on around them. Unlike grey parrots, Amazons have more self-confidence and are not usually so nervous in the company of strangers. Amazons are often good mimics of human speech but however enticing the idea of a talking parrot is, this should not be the main reason for acquiring an Amazon. Even Amazons bred in captivity remain essentially wild birds in that they are not domesticated creatures as are many other companion animals. Amazons retain all their wild-type behavioral needs and, wherever possible, this has to be allowed for if your bird is to have a good life in captivity. As can be appreciated from the previous chapter, the life of wild Amazons is very different from the life we ask them to lead in captivity. But when companion birds are kept so that they can carry out as many of their wild-type behaviors in captivity as possible, including daily periods of flight, then they can adapt well to living with us.

Much out-of-cage time is needed

While Amazons may display a degree of confidence not seen in some other parrots, they are still flock animals, designed to live in social groups. Wild Amazons are highly vulnerable to being preyed upon by a range of other creatures, including humans, but life in a flock affords them good protection from predators. With this in mind, companion Amazons will still be cautious about unfamiliar objects or actions going on around them and they may be suspicious of seemingly harmless things. So care needs to be taken when introducing new objects or people to an Amazon. They are intelligent and generally rather busy birds, so they need to be kept occupied. Providing a range of toys (see pages 46-7), particularly ones which they can chew up to destruction, helps keep them occupied, but it is vital that Amazons are not confined to a cage for long periods of the day. They need many hours out of the cage so they can interact with you and the rest of your family. An Amazon parrot should not be thought of as an easy-maintenance pet. They will need a lot of attention every day.

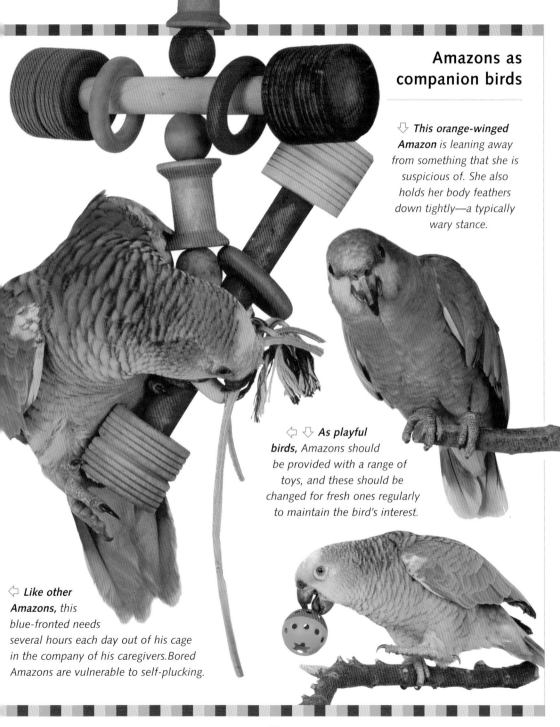

Amazons as companion birds

⇩ **This orange-winged Amazon** is leaning away from something that she is suspicious of. She also holds her body feathers down tightly—a typically wary stance.

⇦ ⇩ **As playful birds,** Amazons should be provided with a range of toys, and these should be changed for fresh ones regularly to maintain the bird's interest.

⇦ **Like other Amazons,** this blue-fronted needs several hours each day out of his cage in the company of his caregivers. Bored Amazons are vulnerable to self-plucking.

The importance of rearing

As with any immature animal, young Amazons show submissive behaviors and are often sold as "cuddle-tame" birds. These submissive behaviors are an adaptation which tells other birds that they are harmless and pose no threat, so they are treated gently by other adult birds. However, by the time Amazons are two or three years old their baby behaviors will have

⇦ **The dark eye** reveals this to be a young bird.

been replaced with a more assertive approach to life. This change in their behavior often comes as a surprise to their human companions, but it is quite normal, indeed predictable. Some Amazons become one-person birds, overbonding to one person only. They may reject having anything to do with anyone else other than their favored person. However, the tendency for this to happen can be reduced by suitable training, as discussed later.

Different methods used to raise young birds

The quality of an Amazon as a pet bird is, however, greatly affected by how they are raised. Most parrots produced for the pet trade are now captive-bred. Captive-bred birds may be hand-reared, parent-reared, or part-parent-reared. There are major differences in the behavior of these birds when they mature, depending on which of these methods was used to raise them. Birds which have never seen their own parents and have been hand-reared from the day they hatched can present special problems as adult birds. These birds are very prone to being overdependent on one person and they are more likely to experience behavioral problems such as self-plucking and excessive screaming. Having missed out on the normal interactions with their own natural parents, they don't see themselves as parrots, but identify purely with humans for all their needs. They often lack confidence in new situations. With their very submissive behaviors as babies, these birds are much easier to sell.

Parent-raised birds make the best 'pets'

Conversely, parent-raised Amazons are less tame as babies but develop into adults that show more normal behaviors. They also have more confidence and, importantly, a degree of independence that renders them less prone to behavioral problems and overbonding with one person. Part-parent-raised birds are those which have been raised by their parents for a few weeks, at least until their eyes have opened, but have then been hand-reared. The behavior of these birds as adults falls somewhere between the other two types and they can do quite well as pet birds. Hand-reared birds are far more commonly available than parent- or part-parent-raised birds. However, if you can obtain a parent- or part-parent-raised Amazon, these usually make better companion birds.

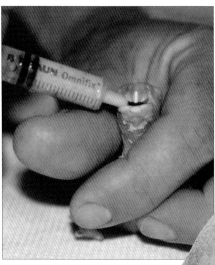

▷ **These white-fronted Amazons** are about 25 days old. Their eyes have been open for several days already.

⇧ **At seven weeks old,** these green-cheeked Amazons will soon be ready to exercise their wings and try flying.

⇧ **This four-day-old Amazon** is being hand-reared; parent-rearing would be better for the bird!

⇧ **Though capable of feeding himself,** this mealy Amazon still enjoys being hand-fed. Large species can take many months to become food independent.

Amazons as part of the family

Whatever Amazon you choose to have, you should be aware that these birds have very loud voices. It is part of their normal adult behavior to engage in regular screaming sessions each day. These sessions usually last for less than 30 minutes and tend to occur in the early morning and again in the late afternoon. There may be additional screaming sessions when the bird is overexcited. Such screaming sessions are not a behavioral problem, though some people mistakenly consider them to be so. It is quite normal for Amazons to be loud birds!

Take care with children and birds

The larger Amazons, such as the blue-fronted,

⇧ *Amazon parrots should not be allowed access to the shoulder, especially a child's shoulder, as they can inflict painful bites.*

mealy, and yellow-naped, have powerful beaks, and these birds are capable of inflicting serious injuries, particularly on children. Such injuries are rare, but if you are considering an Amazon and you have young children, you might find it best to choose one of the smaller species, such as the red-lored, white-fronted, or perhaps an orange-winged Amazon. Amazons will need lots of attention each day out of the cage, but as adults, some are inclined to become over-excited. In most cases, this arises when the people around the bird are also overexcited or gesticulating and the bird just wants to join in. As soon as the mood in the room changes and everyone calms down, so does the bird as well. So you can certainly influence the bird's behavior quite easily by how you and your family behave when in the company of the bird.

Amazons can do well in a fairly busy house-hold, but the importance of training the bird to accept some basic requests or commands from you and everyone who wants to interact with the bird needs to be appreciated. This training is discussed later. A well-trained Amazon can be a joy to be with, but the very same bird who has not been trained can be difficult to keep well as a companion animal. Adult male Amazons often show aggressive behaviors, but only seasonally; typically each year during the spring for one or two months. Extra care should be taken in handling a bird in this condition until the behavior subsides. Again, the smaller Amazons, such as the white-fronted and red-lored, are easier to cope with regarding this aspect of their natural behavior.

▷ **Red-lored Amazons,** though not as commonly seen as pets as some other species, are popular companion birds.

⇧ **White-fronted Amazons** have an outgoing, playful character.

◁ **While some Amazons can** become one-person birds, this is not generally a problem with these parrots.

Most biting is caused by ⇨ misunderstandings between a bird and its caregivers but children should be closely supervised when with them.

Acquiring an Amazon: what t

While pet shops and some garden centers might seem the most obvious sources for getting an Amazon parrot, there are other places to try. You can check breeders' adverts in birdkeeping journals and avian publications, and buy direct from the breeder rather than a shop. Some breeders may let you visit their premises where you can take the time over several visits to get to know more about parrots before making your

⇦ *Buying a bird from a pet shop is one of several options.*

final choice. Private ads appear in local newspapers as well, often with older birds being offered. While some businesses advertise birds on the Internet, you should always make sure you visit the seller to see the bird in its current home and establish that you trust the seller before acquiring the bird. Also, make sure that you have some form of guarantee as to the bird's health before parting with your money and get a detailed receipt for your bird which includes date of purchase, the species of bird, and any identification on the bird, such as a band or microchip.

Give a home to an unwanted bird

As is the case with other pets, there are actually far more parrots around than there are good homes for them to go to, and many birds end up in rescue centers and sanctuaries. Some

of these places do foster their birds out to suitable homes. Some parrots from these places may have behavioral problems, and this may have been the reason why they were given to a sanctuary in the first place. But if an older bird has always been a pet bird, you may be able to offer it better one-to-one attention than staff at a sanctuary are able to provide. To find details of these sources, you can search the Internet using the search terms "parrot sanctuary," or "parrot rescue" or "parrot rehoming," etc. Or you could contact the ASPCA—or in the UK, the RSPCA and—ask them for details of bona fide sources of birds in need of good homes.

Birds are sometimes described as being tame but later prove not to be. If a bird is advertised as tame, make sure you see the seller handling the bird and confirm that it is comfortable with being handled, even if this is only stepping up and down on request. When buying a bird, it is a case of "let the buyer beware," so take your time when choosing an Amazon.

It is best to ensure a ⇨
bird advertised as tame really is comfortable with being handled, at least by the seller.

⇧ **Birds in pet stores** which are out of their cages may be wing-clipped. This sometimes causes behavioral problems, so take care when considering such a bird.

You can find ⇨
sources of birds on the Internet. However, you should always see the bird in its home before buying it.

Signs of health and sickness

Like many birds, Amazons try to hide any signs of being unhealthy and try to appear normal. They can do this right up to the point when they become seriously ill, so you need to be able to recognize a healthy bird by looking for the telltale signs of good health. Healthy birds are active for most, but not all, of the daytime. The eyes should be bright and wide open. There should be no discharge from the nostrils, and the breathing should be silent. The bird should be alert and appear well aware of things going on around it. The body feathers should be in good condition. They should not be fluffed up, nor held down with an excessive tightness but just relaxed and slightly smoothed down. The bird should be eating normally and passing droppings normally without excessive straining. The area around the vent should be clean, not soiled by droppings. When at rest or sleeping, a healthy bird usually stands on one foot.

Look out for signs of ill health

Birds that are sick will show the opposite of these signs: fluffed-up feathers, an inattentive, sleepy disposition, with dull, perhaps half-closed eyes. They may sleep while standing on both feet instead of one foot only. When you see an Amazon that does not display the normal healthy signs, something may be wrong, so take great care if you are considering purchasing such a bird. You can always ask the owner to have the bird checked by a specialist avian vet before you buy it and see the vet's report. It is certainly worth having a vet check done within a day or two of acquiring any bird.

Remember, immature birds are often described as "cuddle-tame" but such submissive behaviors are only a temporary feature related to the bird's age. A bird's adult behaviors can be very different from those seen while it is immature. So there is an advantage in getting an older bird (generally from a private sale or parrot rehoming service) in that the bird's true character will be well-formed and there is unlikely to be any major change to this subsequently. While older birds are often sold for genuine reasons, many are also sold because their owners are having problems with the bird they cannot cope with. The most common of these are high noise levels, nervousness, and aggression, so ask about these aspects of the bird's character as well. Often, these behavioral problems are not difficult to address and remedy, as is discussed later.

⇧ *While this bird's feathers are fluffed up,* the eye is alert and the bird appears well aware of things that are going on around him.

⇦ *Conversely, this orange-winged Amazon* has a dull, sunken eye and seems utterly inattentive. This bird could certainly be unwell.

⇦ *Note the poor feather condition* of this Amazon, and the fact that the feathers are slightly fluffed up; these are signs that this bird may not be well.

Displaced feathers to the ⇧ *"thumb;"* this indicates that the bird's wing may be damaged.

CHAPTER 4

The sense of sight

As with other parrots, an Amazon's keenest sense is its sight. These birds have a number of adaptations to their eyes which greatly improve their vision compared to human sight. The part of the eye that you can see is only a small part of the eyeball itself, which is much larger. The skull of a bird reveals its eye sockets which show the true size of the eyes. All parrot's eyes are arranged to give them almost 360-degree, all-round vision, both vertically and horizontally. This ensures they can easily spot danger, such as a hawk which may attack from any direction. They also have good binocular or stereo vision as we do, for objects which are relatively near and in front of them. All parrots can switch back and forth between their all-round monocular vision to close-up stereo vision in a split second. Parrots' eyes are somewhat flattened, not spherical like ours, so they have limited eye-movement within the socket. Instead, they tend to move the whole head when looking at objects. Parrots also have a third eyelid which you can sometimes see when the bird blinks.

Enhanced color vision

While human color vision is limited to mixes of red, green, and blue light in the visible spectrum, parrots also see ultraviolet light as another one, perhaps even two, distinct colors. This may help them distinguish between the sexes, as some color differences between males and females may only be apparent in UV colors. UV vision may also help them identify from a distance the fruits they commonly eat and

determine if they are ripe. Unlike humans, parrots have voluntary control of their iris, and can open and close their pupils rapidly at will. This ability to flash their eyes is used to express excitement or to threaten another bird.

Birds process visual information at a much faster rate than we do. Our brain takes in about 16 images per second from our eyes. This is why a film projected at around 25 frames per second gives us the illusion of a moving image. Birds, however, can take in up to 170 images per second. This ability to process more information per second probably helps them to see well when flying at high speed through the trees. Parrots are very sensitive to moving objects and your bird may be frightened by seemingly harmless things, such as a broom or dustpan when these are being used, so take care to avoid frightening your bird with unfamiliar objects.

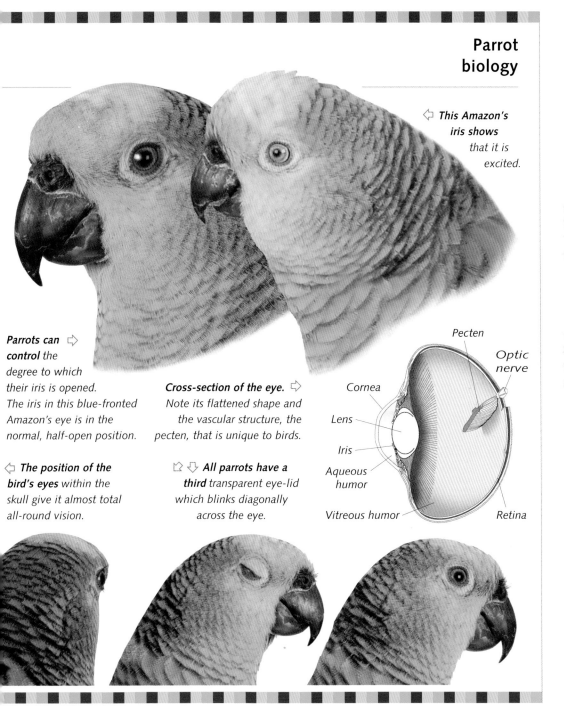

◁ **This Amazon's iris shows** that it is excited.

Parrots can ⇨ **control** the degree to which their iris is opened. The iris in this blue-fronted Amazon's eye is in the normal, half-open position.

◁ **The position of the bird's eyes** within the skull give it almost total all-round vision.

Cross-section of the eye. ⇨ Note its flattened shape and the vascular structure, the pecten, that is unique to birds.

⇗ ⇩ **All parrots have a third** transparent eye-lid which blinks diagonally across the eye.

Pecten
Optic nerve
Cornea
Lens
Iris
Aqueous humor
Vitreous humor
Retina

Hearing, touch, temperature an

A bird does not have an external visible ear—the opening to the ears lies just below and behind the eyes. The feathers covering the ear are sparse and allow sound waves to pass through easily. A parrot's ears work in much the same way as our ears; they are used not only to hear a similar range of sounds but to maintain balance. Vibrations of air caused

Position of ear

Fluid-filled semi-circular canals

The semi- ⇨
circular canals Middle ear
which aid balance
comprise three Inner ear
fluid-filled loops.

by sound pass down the open ear tube to the eardrum. Here, these vibrations are passed through a tiny bone to the inner fluid-filled ear, which acts like a microphone, sending electrical signals to the brain dozens of times per second.

Parrots have an arrangement of three fluid-filled semi-circular canals in each inner ear which detect movement and gravity. This apparatus sends signals to the bird's brain to ensure both balance and correct attitude of the body during flight. Despite the banking, diving,

and rolling movements birds use in flight, these semicircular canals allow them to keep their heads as level as possible at all times, no matter what the bird's position is in the air.

A muscular, sensitive tongue

The whole of a bird's body is sensitive to touch and temperature through the skin. This includes disturbance to feathers, light touching, air pressure, and pain. Two areas are particularly sensitive to touch for parrots: the tongue and the feet. Parrots are perhaps unique among birds in the way they use their tongue. The first contact with some new food or object is often with the front of the beak which is used to prod it, perhaps to see if it is safe; then the tongue is used much like a fingertip to feel it. All parrots' tongues are very muscular as well as sensitive to temperature and texture. The tongue is used to find the weakest point in nuts and seeds before cracking them open. Parrots experience a similar range of tastes as us, but they have no sensitivity to hot peppers! Most of their taste buds are not on the tongue itself but on the roof of the mouth to which the tongue transfers minute quantities of food to be tested before deciding whether to swallow it.

A parrot's feet are very sensitive to touch, particularly vibrations. This allows them to be aware of anything which might be crawling along their branch or perch at night when vision is very limited. The bird is aware of which side of their branch the disturbance comes from and can take evasive action if needed. Parrots do not seem to have a good sense of smell.

aste

The bird uses the highly ⇨
sensitive upper surface of its
tongue to test the texture and
taste of a peanut before cracking
it open for a second time.

◁ *The undersurface
of a parrot's toes are
very sensitive to touch
and also to vibrations.
Parrots are at risk
from nocturnal
predators but their
eyesight at night is
quite poor. However,
the sensitivity of their
feet ensures that they
can detect possible
predators trying to
approach them.*

Breathing and blood circulatio

As with all flying birds, Amazon parrots have respiratory and circulatory systems that have evolved to enable them to fly at high speed and over considerable distances without the bird becoming tired. Oxygen in fresh air is used to burn the bird's fuel, which is the food it has broken down in its digestive tract. This fuel is used for bodily functions, such as keeping warm and of course powering the muscles for the bird's range of activities including flight. While flight is an extremely efficient way of getting about (much more efficient than walking), it is very demanding in terms of energy use. But Amazons can breathe at rates which would amount to hyperventilation in other animals and they are adapted to this "high-octane" performance. The waste products of this activity, mainly carbon dioxide and water, are also eliminated at elevated rates.

Efficient metabolism

In terms of effort, the difference between a bird walking and then flying is a bit like the difference between a car trundling around in first gear and then being driven at high speed in top gear. In addition to their lungs, which are similar to ours, birds have a system of air-sacs throughout their bodies. Although these are little more than air-filled bags found throughout the bird's body, by shunting air around these air-sacs at high speed, birds can deliver a *constant* supply of fresh air to the lungs. So the air travels over the lungs in the same direction all the time, rather than just being sucked in and blown out as with our method of breathing and the lungs are permanently inflated. These refinements mean that a bird's breathing abilities are 25 per cent more efficient than ours.

Parrots have a four-chambered heart like ours, and the bird's blood circulatory system works at a high-speed level to match its high-speed breathing Even while at rest, a parrot's heart beats at about 140 times per minute—more than twice the rate of a human heart. When flying, this increases to around 900 beats per minute and this is quite normal for parrots. An Amazon's normal blood temperature is 104-106°F (40-41°C). This temperature is much higher than that found in humans. All these adaptations allow a parrot's body to operate at a much higher rate than mammals of a similar size can do. This is needed to ensure the birds can fly fast and efficiently.

◁ *Parrots use little energy when walking, compared to that used in active, flapping flight. This orange-winged Amazon can fly at around 56kph (35mph) and wild parrots can sustain this for hours if necessary.*

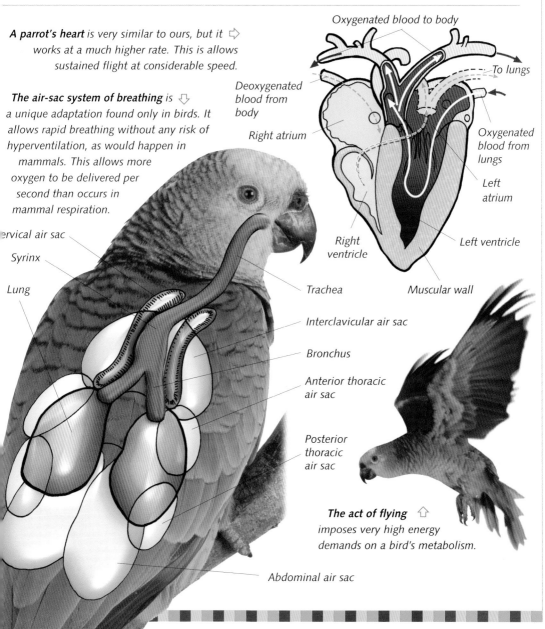

A parrot's heart is very similar to ours, but it ⇨ works at a much higher rate. This is allows sustained flight at considerable speed.

The air-sac system of breathing is ⇩ a unique adaptation found only in birds. It allows rapid breathing without any risk of hyperventilation, as would happen in mammals. This allows more oxygen to be delivered per second than occurs in mammal respiration.

Oxygenated blood to body

Deoxygenated blood from body

To lungs

Right atrium

Oxygenated blood from lungs

Left atrium

ervical air sac

Syrinx

Lung

Right ventricle

Left ventricle

Trachea

Muscular wall

Interclavicular air sac

Bronchus

Anterior thoracic air sac

Posterior thoracic air sac

The act of flying ⇧ imposes very high energy demands on a bird's metabolism.

Abdominal air sac

The digestive system

Amazon parrots are vegetarians, eating a wide range of fruits, flowers, seeds, nuts, and young leaves and shoots. They have a preference for any food of a high nutritional value; this means they tend to favor foods with a high fat content, such as nuts and seeds, or a high sugar content, such as sweet, ripe fruits. An Amazon's beak is a universal tool with sharp cutting edges capable of

*⇦ **Amazons have to learn** how to manipulate things with their feet and this only comes with trial and experience. Young birds acquire these skills in their first few months.*

exerting powerful crushing and cutting forces. The beak is used with great skill in combination with the sensitive and muscular tongue to examine and manipulate items of food. Amazons also use their feet in combination with the beak to hold larger items of food when necessary. Unlike most other birds, parrots use their beak in a chewing action to chop up their food into small pieces before swallowing. They also discard parts of the food which are poor in nutrients, such as the skins of grapes and seed coats, by using the beak to peel this off before swallowing the more nutritious parts.

Rapid digestion

The food then passes into the bird's crop. The crop is an extension of the esophagus, where food is stored before the next stages of digestion. It then passes to the proventriculus, a part of the bird's stomach where proper digestion begins as digestive juices are secreted and mixed with the food. Next food passes to the gizzard. This is a highly muscular part of the stomach where food is ground down under great pressure by a grinding action. The inner surface of the gizzard is as rough as sandpaper, and the physical crushing of food here renders it into a fine paste. The food then passes into the

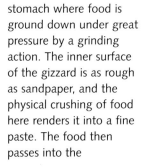

duodenum and the intestines where the well-digested nutrients are passed into the bloodstream. It is these nutrients which, when combined with oxygen, provide the fuel needed for all the bird's bodily functions.

Water is recycled

Indigestible items and waste products are voided via the cloaca. Parrots retain and recycle as much water as their bodies need, so they do not pass large quantities of watery urine as mammals do. Instead, they excrete urea as the white part of the droppings, again via the cloaca. Since a parrot's digestive tract is very short and birds have higher body temperatures, food is usually completely digested within a few minutes and the waste products are also excreted rapidly.

◁ **Given a choice of foods,** Amazons will generally pick high fat items. This orange-winged chooses a peanut, which is 46 percent fat. Captive birds should receive a restricted amount of these fatty foods.

◁ **When eating fruits and vegetables,** the bird's droppings will be wetter; this is quite normal and nothing to worry about.

⇩ **The digestive tract of parrots** is quite short; if spread out, it would be about three times the length of the bird. Parrots do not waste energy trying to digest nutrient-poor parts of any seeds or fruits they find. They remove any unwanted husks and shells and concentrate only on the nutrient-rich parts.

Esophagus

Crop

Esophagus

Proventriculus

Gizzard

Supraduodenal loop

Duodenum

Cloaca

CHAPTER 5

How Amazon parrots fly

Amazons are essentially flying creatures and this is their normal way of getting about. Flying for parrots is as natural as walking is for us. Flying birds never carry any "excess baggage," so almost every cell in their body is modified to reduce weight while retaining strength. Birds have light hollow bones, very light feathers, and little or no fat. They also have a powerful engine—the massive pectoral muscles and large heart to enable sustained flight for hours if necessary.

The slightly curved shape of the bird's wings generates lift. As air flows over the wings it results in the wings (and therefore the bird!) being pushed upwards. The faster the air flows over the wings, the greater the force of lift. The outer half of the bird's wing, the ten primary feathers, provide the propulsion needed to ensure this airflow is maintained. As the bird flaps downwards and backwards, air is pushed backwards over the wings. In addition to gravity, the main limiting factor in sustained flight is the friction that occurs between the bird and the air, called *drag*. However, the bird's very streamlined shape helps to minimize drag.

The different forms of flight

There are several forms of flight. In powered flight, the wings beat regularly and the bird is able to climb easily and rapidly in the air. The 'cruising' speed of Amazons is around 35 to 45mph (56 to 72kph) and they can sustain this for hours if necessary. Thus, wild Amazons can cover huge distances during a brief time on the wing. This flapping flight is expensive in terms of energy use, but the bird's whole body is very well adapted to the demands of flying.

Amazons can also glide but this is usually confined to the point where the bird is coming in to land. Here, the bird ceases to flap but keeps the wings held out as it moves forward. Since gliding is passive, it results in a loss of height. Eventually the bird must either land or switch its engine on again and return to flapping flight to regain lift. Amazons can also hover, turn 360° on the spot, and stall at the point of landing as they put their feet out to grip the perch. The whole of the bird's body and wings are used for each flying task. While the primaries are used for propulsion, they are also used in steering and as air-brakes when employing a reverse-thrust action on landing. The tail helps with steering and acts as a horizontal flap for deceleration on landing.

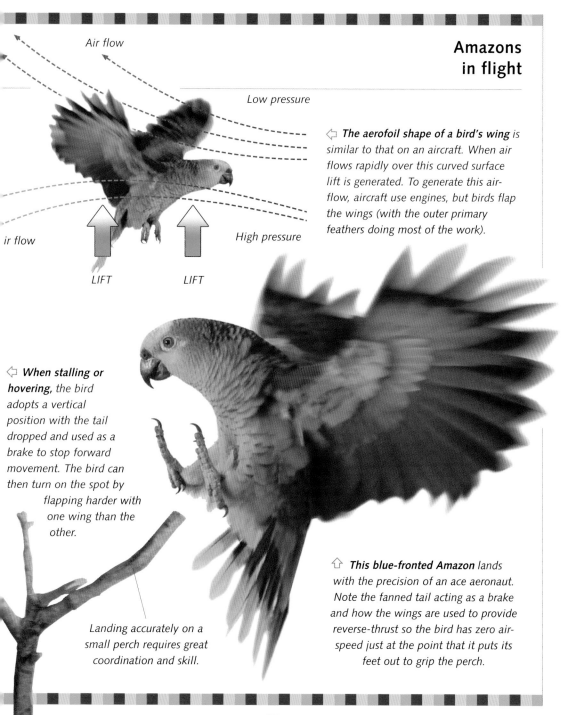

Air flow

Low pressure

⇦ **The aerofoil shape of a bird's wing** *is similar to that on an aircraft. When air flows rapidly over this curved surface lift is generated. To generate this air-flow, aircraft use engines, but birds flap the wings (with the outer primary feathers doing most of the work).*

ir flow

High pressure

LIFT   LIFT

⇦ **When stalling or hovering,** *the bird adopts a vertical position with the tail dropped and used as a brake to stop forward movement. The bird can then turn on the spot by flapping harder with one wing than the other.*

Landing accurately on a small perch requires great coordination and skill.

⇧ **This blue-fronted Amazon** *lands with the precision of an ace aeronaut. Note the fanned tail acting as a brake and how the wings are used to provide reverse-thrust so the bird has zero air-speed just at the point that it puts its feet out to grip the perch.*

How Amazons learn to fly

Baby Amazons normally leave the nest (fledge) at 9 to 12 weeks old but remain highly dependent on their parents for their food and safety for many more months. On first leaving the nest, the fledglings make their first attempts to fly. While the *urge* to fly is very strong in the birds at this age, their *abilities* to fly are very poor. This is because the skills of flying have to be learned by each bird through simple trial and error experiences. Young birds will practise flapping while perched. This helps to strengthen their pectoral muscles (the main muscles used to fly) and gives them the feel of the power of their wings and the lift this generates. Soon they gain the confidence to take off for their first flight but usually they crash-land clumsily. However, after a few days their abilities to maneuver and control their speed and direction while airborne begins to improve and they soon land with more precision.

The importance of learning to fly

In captive-bred parrots, it is vital to encourage these youngsters to fly at this stage. This ensures the birds develop normally and that their muscles, including the heart, also develop normally. Where such young birds are denied the opportunities to learn to fly, they often fail to learn to fly properly for the rest of their lives. This in itself can cause the birds to develop behavioral problems as they are unable to escape from things which frighten them by flying off. Instead, they may become so-called "phobic" birds with an exaggerated fear of harmless objects or actions.

In the wild, birds try to face into wind when taking off just as aircraft do, since the faster the air moves over the wings, the more free lift the birds get. Captive birds rarely have this advantage, and it can take them longer to learn to fly well indoors where space tends to be very limited and there is no wind to help point them in the right direction when taking off and landing. However, after a few weeks, most captive-bred birds will have developed their flying techniques very well and become adept at using these skills.

⇧ *More of an Amazon's colors* can be seen when the bird opens its wings.

◁ **This bird ducks down** and opens its wings as it prepares to take off. The bird will then jump clear of the perch so as not to catch his wings on the perch during the first downstroke. For young birds, taking off is easy, it's landing which has to be practiced carefully.

Small muscles in the wing adjust the angle and direction of the wing-stroke.

Extensors

Biceps

Forearm muscles

Triceps

Latissimus dorsi

Supracoracoideus (raises wing)

Ilio tibialis

Pectoralis (pulls wing down)

Ilio fibularis

Gastrocnemius

The main flight muscles are ⇧ found in the chest; these pull the wings down rapidly and a separate pair are used to raise the wings.

Safety in the home

There are two aspects to bear in mind regarding the safety of your bird while it is out of the cage. First, you should be aware of how to avoid common household dangers and second, you should recognize the advantage of training your bird to accept some flight requests from you (see pages 62-5).

⇲ *Large mirrors should be removed or covered over, and any large windows concealed behind opaque curtains.*

Windows and external doors should be kept closed *before* you ask your bird to come out of the cage. Alternatively, you can cover windows with a guard or mesh which allows them to be open, but prevents the bird from escaping. Any large windows in rooms where your bird is allowed to fly should be covered with curtains to prevent the bird thinking it can fly through the glass. Large mirrors are confusing and dangerous for birds, so these should be removed. Ceiling fans can cause a fearful reaction in some birds as the blades may be seen as a predator's wings, so birds should not have access to rooms with fans in them. The kitchen presents many dangers to birds including very hot surfaces and electrical appliances, so it's best to avoid having birds here. Birds may also drown if they fall into a toilet or any other water container.

Introduce your bird to any new room

When encouraging a bird to use an unfamiliar room and to fly in that room, make sure that you introduce the bird to the room carefully. Without this introduction, the bird will not know which places are safe and suitable to land on. This introductory stage requires a fairly formal training period when the bird is asked to step down onto places you would like him to go to and is then given a reward, perhaps a food treat, for doing so. Suitable places could include chair backs, the sofa, window ledges, tabletops, and a stand for the bird. When doing this for the first time, only allow the bird to stay on a new place for a *few seconds*, then ask him to step back onto your hand. After the bird has been introduced to these places as perches, when he does fly, he will be much less likely to crash-land and will have more confidence around the room.

If your bird is ever suddenly frightened of something and takes flight and crash-lands, do *not* approach him until a few moments have passed and he has collected his senses. If you approach a frightened bird too readily, he will associate you with the fearful incident and may become very afraid of you and your hands.

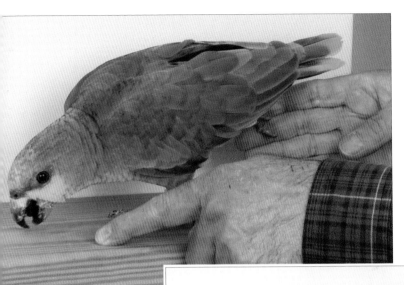

⇦ *Don't leave a bird* to explore a new room on his own. Take time to introduce the bird to those places you wish him to use as perches. Ask him to 'Go down' on several places and reward him when he does so.

⇩ *After a few sessions* of this reward-based training, most birds get used to the new room.

⇩ *If a bird crash-lands,* do *not* approach him immediately. Instead, wait until he recovers himself and then ask him to come towards *you*.

CHAPTER 6

Choosing the right cage

While it is very likely that a companion parrot will generally be housed in a cage, the amount of time your bird spends there each day will have a great effect on its quality of life and behavior. For your bird to remain physically and mentally well, he will need to spend many hours out of the cage each day where he can interact with you, and other people and/or other birds.

The cage should large enough so that the bird can easily flap its wings while it is inside. So the main factor in deciding on the minimum cage size for your bird is the bird's wingspan.

⇧ *An orange-winged Amazon is measured for wingspan. The measurement between the center of this bird's back and a wing tip is 12in (30cm).*

The wingspan is the measurement from wingtip to wing tip when the bird's wings are fully outstretched, as though it were in flight. This varies with the species of Amazon. Smaller Amazons, such as the white-fronted, have a wingspan of about 21in (53cm). The blue-fronted and yellow-headed measure up to 28in (71cm) and the mealy and yellow-naped are over 30in (76cm). A cage in which the height, depth, and width all exceed the bird's wingspan will allow the bird to flap its wings. The *width* and *depth* of the cage are far more important considerations than its height since the bird will only use the top half of the cage anyway.

Choose a large, well-constructed strong cage
While the best and most expensive cages are made of plain stainless steel, most are made of mild steel which is then coated with various layers of paint. The paintwork is usually stove-enamelled. This process hardens the paint and ensures that it cannot be damaged or removed by the bird. The bars should be sufficiently thick and strong enough that the bird cannot bend or damage them. Damaged bars can result in the protective coating being chewed away by the bird. Parrots enjoy being able to climb and this allows some exercise. To aid this, the cage should have horizontal, as well as vertical, bars. For the bird's safety, the spacing between the bars should be no more than 1in (2.5cm); this prevents the bird from poking its head out between the bars. It is an advantage to choose a cage with the food bowls mounted on swing feeders which allows the food to be changed from outside the cage. The sliding tray on the base should be made of metal rather than plastic to avoid it being damaged by the bird.

⇧ ⇩ *Swing feeders allow you to change the bird's food from outside the cage. This can be useful if you are away and someone else needs to feed your bird.*

This cage is of sound ⇨ construction and has suitable bar spacing for a fully grown Amazon parrot.

Setting up the cage

As cages are usually made with wire on all four sides, without a solid rear wall, the cage should always be positioned with its back against a wall in the room. This will give the bird a greater feeling of security. Also, if possible, position the cage so the bird can see out of a window, perhaps onto your garden where the comings and goings of other birds will add some interest for your bird. Make sure, however, that the cage is never in full sun as the bird can very easily become overheated. The cage should be high enough so that the top perches allow the bird to be at your eye level when you are standing next to the cage. If the bird is nervous, the height of the top perch should be increased, so that the bird can look down on you. If the cage has a grill just above its floor-tray, this should be removed as it prevents the bird having access to the floor. The cage floor should be covered with sheets of newspaper which are changed each day.

⇧ **Parrots may feel fearful** if all sides of their cage are exposed. All-wire cages can have a cloth draped over the back to help the bird feel more secure inside.

a locking mechanism in their feet when perched which allows them to grip the perch with little effort, but this does not work on thick perches. For Amazons, the most comfortable (top) perch should be about ¾in (20mm) in diameter. This allows the bird to wrap its toes almost right around the perch. Other perches can be thicker or thinner. Perches made from any natural untreated hardwood, such as ash, hawthorn, maple, hazel and cherry are suitable. Rope perches of natural fibers, such as cotton, jute or hemp, are also beneficial.

Softwood perches should be avoided; the bird can destroy these within a few minutes and softwood often has a glue-like resin which will stick to bird's feathers. Plastic perches should be avoided as well. Most birds will chew their perches, and this helps them exercise their beak. With this in mind perches should be seen as disposable items to be renewed frequently. Since they get dirty very easily, it is useful to have two sets of perches for each cage so you always have a spare set when needed. Sometimes an abrasive perch is used to keep a bird's claws less sharp. But all parrots need fairly sharp claws to grip smooth surfaces properly. If you use an abrasive perch, this should be placed low down in the cage and not be the bird's favorite or top perch.

Use perches of natural wood

To ensure the bird's feet are exercised properly, there should be a variety of perches in the cage and these should be of differing thickness. Usually, perches supplied with a new cage are of uniform and excessive thickness. Parrots have

⇐ *If an abrasive perch is used, it should be fitted low down in the cage.*

⇩ *This perch is too thick for the foot-locking mechanism to work. The bird could not sleep comfortably on it.*

This thinner ⇩
perch allows the foot-locking mechanism to work well. The toes grip tight.

Muscles

Ankle joint

As the bird squats, this tendon is pulled tight causing the toes to grip the perch.

⇧ *When standing,* a bird uses more energy in its leg muscles. If a perch is too thick, the bird is forced to stand and cannot grip the perch passively.

Furnishing the cage

To keep your parrot mentally stimulated, the cage should be made as interesting as possible, so the way in which you furnish the cage is very important to your bird. A great variety of toys are available for parrots now, principally in two different types: hanging toys and smaller foot toys. Hanging toys are more permanent than foot toys, though these will often be destroyed eventually as the bird chews them. You should aim to position two or three hanging toys in the cage at a time, but to keep your bird interested and entertained, you should maintain a collection of toys and change one around every few days.

Foot toys are those small enough for the bird to hold in his foot. These are often a bird's favorite toys and foot toys are usually designed to be destructible, rather than long lasting. While there are lots of commercially available foot toys to be found in pet shops, you can often make or obtain these for little or no cost. Suitable items include pine cones, small cardboard boxes, clothespins, lollipop sticks, pieces of twisted newspaper, small hardwood sticks, small hard plastic balls and some puzzle toys. You can put food treats into the puzzle toys, and your bird can be left to work out how it is going to extract them.

Safety issues

Toys must be safe for your bird to play with, so avoid any with small or sharp metal parts that might be detached and swallowed by the bird. Any cord used as a fastening should be kept very short to prevent the bird becoming entangled in it. Take care with any rings used. Rings should either be so small that the bird cannot get its head through them, *or* so large that the bird's whole body can pass easily through. If the bird gets aggressive or overexcited when given a mirror, this should be removed.

It helps also to provide your bird with a roosting box in the cage to give him somewhere to hide away and to sleep in. Amazons will usually remain silent when in the box. The box should be made from ¾in (19mm) plywood and be big enough so the bird can turn around while inside. For most Amazons, the internal measurements should be about 12in (30cm) square by 7in (18cm) high. Smaller species can have a smaller box and larger Amazons, such as mealys and yellow-naped, will need a box 14in (36cm) square by 8in (20cm) high. Make the entrance hole quite large and fit the box securely, high up in the cage. Put a layer of wood shavings on the floor to a depth of about 1.5in (40mm). You can also put some chewable toys inside to keep the bird occupied.

◁ *Small chew-toys which can be held in the foot and chewed to destruction are often an Amazon's most favored toys.*

⇩ *Hanging toys should be* introduced carefully. It helps if the bird can see you playing with any new toy a few times before it is taken anywhere near the cage.

⇧ *A roosting box* should have a large entrance hole so you can ask the bird to come out if necessary. It should be placed high up in the cage.

Small balls or other ⇨ *small foot toys* with parts within them that rattle often intrigue a parrot. The bird will try to dismantle the toy. If it contains a food treat, this is all the more rewarding.

Parrot stands and an aviary

While your bird is out of its cage, there should be a several places he can fly to and use. These might include chair backs, window ledges, tabletops etc. But your bird should also have at least one stand on which he can play with toys and eat some food while he is out. Stands come in a range of sizes. Get one with several different perches and which can also hold food bowls and has plenty of room for fitting toys onto it. In addition to these large stands, you can also obtain small, portable tabletop stands. You can carry these around with you from one room to another. Amazons like to use a perch rather than having to stand on a flat surface, and these are ideal; most Amazons take to them very easily.

The benefits of a day-flight aviary

If you can provide your bird with an outdoor aviary, this will be of great value to him. The aviary can be used as a day flight, so you just put your bird out during the daytime when the weather is fine and bring him back in before dusk. The aviary can be used even in winter on fine mild days. Birds which have access to the world outdoors have much better feather condition than indoor-kept birds, so allowing your bird to feel the wind and even some rain on his back from time to time will improve the feather condition.

To encourage flight the aviary should be at least 8ft (2.4m) long; the height should be at least 6ft (1.8m). If you make the back higher, you can accommodate a sloping roof which allows water to drain off. The aviary should be made from 1in (2.5cm) square, 14-gauge, best quality welded mesh (gauge is the thickness of the wire). You can use a wooden or metal frame. If a wooden frame is chosen, use 2in or 3in (5cm or 7.5cm) square timbers and hang the mesh on the inside as this gives some protection against the bird chewing the wood. The back of the aviary should be made of some solid, opaque sheeting so that the bird feels more secure. Part

⇧ *An aviary containing* a range of places *that the bird can use allows it to be more active and encourages it to fly as well.*

of the aviary should also be sheltered from rain and direct sun, so use some opaque rigid plastic sheeting for part of the roof.

The aviary floor can be concrete or gravel or left as natural grass. Furnish the aviary with plenty of perches, rope swings and toys and have swing-feeders fitted as well for your bird's feed. Introduce the bird to the aviary in the same way you introduce him to a new room (see page 40).

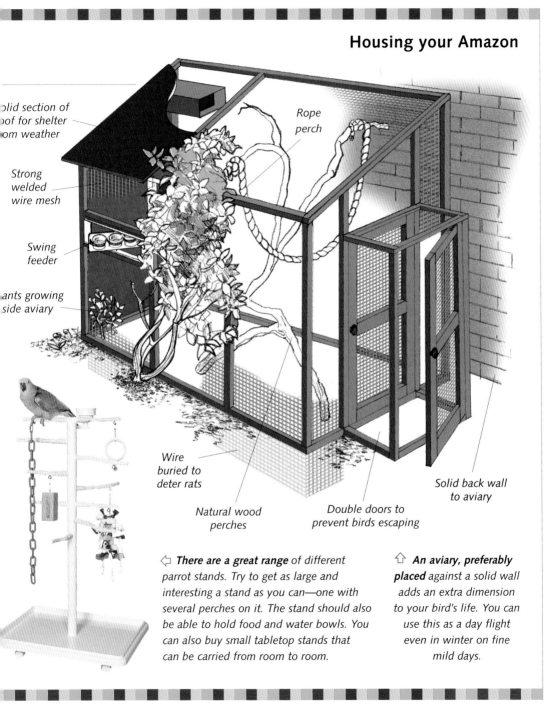

olid section of
oof for shelter
om weather

Rope
perch

Strong
welded
wire mesh

Swing
feeder

ants growing
side aviary

Wire
buried to
deter rats

Natural wood
perches

Double doors to
prevent birds escaping

Solid back wall
to aviary

⇦ **There are a great range** of different
parrot stands. Try to get as large and
interesting a stand as you can—one with
several perches on it. The stand should also
be able to hold food and water bowls. You
can also buy small tabletop stands that
can be carried from room to room.

⇧ **An aviary, preferably
placed** against a solid wall
adds an extra dimension
to your bird's life. You can
use this as a day flight
even in winter on fine
mild days.

CHAPTER 7

What foods are available?

The usual parrot food is a sunflower-seed-based mixture and is not suitable as the main diet for Amazon parrots. This food is nearly 50 percent fat and seriously lacking in important vitamins and minerals. Many Amazons kept on such a diet will develop chronic health problems due to vitamin and mineral deficiencies. This problem of poor diets for captive birds arises because parrots are "programmed" to eat foods of the highest energy value and these are foods high in fat. A wild bird needs a high fat diet as it will be flying hundreds of miles every week and will burn off any excess calories. But a pet parrot is never able exercise at such a rate in one's living room, so the diet for a captive bird needs to reflect that bird's real food needs.

The main ingredients of all foods

Food comprises carbohydrates, fat, and protein; the only other constituents are vitamins, minerals, and water. Grains (cereals such as wheat, rice, and oats) are high in carbohydrates and have good levels of protein as well. Fresh fruits are also high in carbohydrates and these high-energy foods are used by the bird to keep it warm and as a fuel to power the bird's muscles. Nuts and many seeds have high levels of fat being 30 per cent to 80 percent fat. Legumes (peas and beans) are high in protein which is needed to renew and replace body tissues including feathers. For pet parrots, the diet should be mainly carbohydrate (about 75-80 percent) with around 15 percent vegetable protein and only 5-8 percent fat.

In terms of nutrition, it does not matter how these foods are supplied. You can buy pelleted foods formulated specifically for parrots, or alternatively a mixture of fresh natural ingredients. Most pelleted foods are certainly nutritionally well-balanced. However parrots, like humans, appreciate a variety of textures and tastes in their food, and since pellets are of uniform taste and texture, such a diet is seriously lacking in stimulation for the bird. Amazon parrots have a range of techniques for dealing with the different, more natural foods they may encounter and appear to enjoy a range of different healthy foods. So a diet based on fresh fruits, legumes, seeds, and grains adds interest for the bird.

Some human foods, such as chocolate, coffee, tea, alcohol, and avocado, can cause illness or death if eaten by parrots. Salty foods can cause kidney failure, so items such as chips and salty snacks should never be given to any parrot. Parrots should not be given any meat or meat products, either.

Some Amazons prefer seeded grapes, and eat the seeds in preference to the fruit.

⇧ **Most fruits, vegetables, and legumes** *can be given ad lib, as they are low in fat. It is only the nuts and some seeds which should be supplied in a limited quantity.*

⇦ **When given a choice** *of foods, parrots tend to pick out those with the highest fat content first, such as nuts and seeds. Later, the bird will eat the foods with a high sugar or carbohydrate content, such as fruits and legumes.*

Nutritional Values For Some Common Parrot Foods

	Fat	Protein	Carbohydrate
Apple*	0.1%	0.3%	11.5%
Cheese (Cheddar)	34%	25%	0.1%
(Caution: has very high salt content of 1.8%)			
Chickpeas*	5.4%	22%	50%
Maize (corn)*	1%	0.6%	84%
Mixed nuts	64%	16%	4.9%
Peanuts	46%	25%	12%
Pelleted foods*	14%	12%	60%
Pine nuts	69%	8%	11%
Legumes/bean mix*	1.4%	21%	45%
Rice*	1.2%	7.3%	77%
Sunflower seed	48%	12%	18.6%

* indicates the better, low fat foods.
Note: Lost percentages to 100% are mainly composed of water

Nutritious legumes and seeds

Since the nutritional needs of a parrot cannot be satisfied by a dry seed-based diet, and pelleted foods lack stimulation for your bird, it is suggested that you offer a mixture of legumes, fresh fruits and vegetables, and some seeds. Legumes (peas and beans) have to be soaked, and preferably sprouted, in order for them to be edible. The seeds also have a higher nutritional value when soaked and sprouted rather than being fed dry. The following diet is therefore recommended for Amazon parrots.

35 percent soaked/sprouted beans or bean mix (chickpeas are usually the favorite, but you can try black-eye peas, mung beans, or aduki, etc.)

25 percent soaked/sprouted seeds and cereal grains (sunflower, safflower, hemp, millet, wheat, oats, rice, maize etc)

40 percent fresh fruit and vegetables, such as apples, bananas, grapes, pomegranates, carrots, celery, sprouts, green/French beans, peas in the pod, sweet potato, corn-on-the-cob, broccoli etc.

Preparing your bird's food
You might find it easiest to first mix your legumes (35 percent of food) and seed

mixture (25 percent of food) together as a dry food and store it in this way. To prepare it, soak one day's amount of this in water for 12 hours. You can use *warm* but not hot water, as the heat would kill the mixture and prevent it sprouting. The daily amount of food to be soaked will vary from one bird to another with larger birds needing more than smaller Amazons. Usually about 0.7-1.2oz (20-35 grams) of dry food will be enough (its weight will double after soaking). It is quite normal for the beans to smell during this process. After 12 hours you can feed the soaked mixture, but it is best to sprout and germinate the mixture which will occur in the course of another 12 to 24 hours. To do so, just keep the food moist at room temperature (not soaking in water) but rinse it thoroughly several times in cold water to prevent any bacterial contamination of the food. When you see a tiny white shoot appearing, the food is in the best condition to be given to your bird. Don't keep this food for more than one day after it is ready to eat; just throw away all leftovers. Don't cook any bean/seed mixes, nor keep them in a fridge; just feed it raw.

Identical seed and legume ⇨
mixtures; on the left, before soaking, and on the right, spouted and ready to eat.

Feeding your Amazon

Peanuts

Almonds

Cashews

Walnuts

Kiwi fruit

Banana

Apple

In addition to this mixture, the bird should always have fresh fruit and vegetables *every day*. Different birds have their own favoured foods, but try grapes, apple, banana, pomegranate, celery, fresh peas, carrot, etc. When your bird is actually eating a varied diet as described, there is little or no need to supply any other supplements. However, birds kept indoors will not have access to UV light which they need to make use of vitamin D3 in supplying their bodies with calcium. You can overcome this problem by giving a liquid calcium and D3 supplement. Consult your avian veternarian for advice on supplements.

▷ **Providing a range of natural foods** *is an essential form of environmental enrichment for your bird.*

High fat foods, like this walnut, should be fed sparingly, by hand.

Understanding behavior

The main reasons for teaching your bird to accept a few training requests from you are much the same as those for training any animal with which you will be living; you'll need to have good communication with your bird if it is to share your home as a companion animal. A trained Amazon who accepts a few simple requests from you makes a far better companion than a confused, untrained bird who may either be nervous of people or aggressive towards them, due to a lack of basic training. Before you make a start on training, it helps to understand in more detail the motivations that underlie animal behavior in general.

The behaviors of any animal, including ourselves, are always performed for a reason. And the reason is simply that the animal knows it will derive some benefit from doing the behavior. Birds will drink when thirsty and eat when hungry. They will tidy up their feathers by preening until they feel more comfortable. If something frightens a bird, it will move away from it; when it likes something, it will try to move towards it. So, your bird will perform a behavior because it desires the *results* of that behavior.

Reward-based training methods work best

This realization gives us an insight into how to work with a bird and teach it some new behaviors through training. The key is ensuring that you, as your bird's caregiver, always provide your bird with a *reward* for the behaviors that you would like your bird to carry out. The reward is specific to your bird and can be anything which you know your bird *already* really likes; perhaps a small food treat, or having his head scratched, or a favorite toy to play with, or being taken to a favorite place on which to perch. This use of *reward-based training* is central to a proper understanding of your bird's behavior. The study of behavior is called applied behavior analysis (ABA) and the use of methods based on ABA ensures a bird-friendly, cooperative method in working with your bird, rather than the use of any coercive or forceful methods. ABA concentrates on what your bird actually does and how frequently he does these things. While parrots will certainly have their own thoughts and feelings, ABA does not delve into this, since the thoughts and feelings of a parrot cannot be seen or measured in terms of their frequency or intensity.

⇦ *This orange-winged Amazon really appreciates a head-scratch, which can be used as a reward.*

Toys which rattle often intrigue a bird.

⇧ *Some Amazons have favorite toys; these make great rewards as well.*

⇩ *Food rewards work well but you need to experiment to find your own bird's real favorites.*

⇧ *Parrots lead complex lives. We cannot read their minds, but can be guided by their body language.*

Training nervous birds

While Amazons are generally quite bold birds, with more confidence than other kinds of parrots, some individuals can be rather nervous and these birds need to be treated with great care before and during any training. Such nervousness may be due to how other people have handled the bird in the past and parrots have very long memories. Some Amazons may even be wild-caught birds which have been imported as pet birds. Wing-clipping sometimes causes a serious lack of confidence. This may be made worse by the bird being trapped in a cage and unable to escape fearful things happening near it. Before asking a nervous bird to step up onto the hand, you will need to go through a gentle taming process. The same principles of rewarding desired behaviors are used as in the more formal training sessions, but progress with nervous birds may take several weeks. These birds should always have a perch in their cage that is high enough to allow them to be above your eye level when you are standing by the cage. This will reduce the bird's fear of people who come close to it.

Work at a pace which the bird finds comfortable
Start the taming process by sitting down below the bird while it is in its cage but not so close that it shows any signs of nervousness. Sit sideways to the bird and avoid looking directly at it. Let

⇧ *Make sure a nervous bird* can perch above you and sit sideways to the bird. At first you should avoid making eye contact with the bird.

⇧ *As you eat some food yourself,* the bird may become interested in this, so try offering him something through the cage bars as well.

the bird see you doing something such as reading or having a snack to eat. Keep these sessions quite short at first, just two or three minutes, but extend them as the bird gets used to you and gradually sit closer to the bird provided this does not make him nervous. After a few sessions the bird's confidence should improve and he may become interested in any food you may be eating. At this point, offer the bird a favorite tidbit through the bars of the cage.

At later sessions, try opening the cage door and offer a food treat directly to the bird while he is still in the cage. Just place your handheld tidbit below his beak, provided he appears likely to accept this. Later, try leaving the cage door open and offer a treat after the bird has come out or just moved towards the open cage door. To get him to return, tempt him back in with a food treat. Always proceed at a pace which is comfortable for the bird. Use softly spoken words of encouragement as you make progress in this taming stage.

A calm ⇨ *approach* with reward-based training and much patience on your part are the best ways to earn your bird's trust.

⇧ **As the bird's confidence improves,** offer a treat through the open cage door. Initially, you should keep these trust-building sessions quite short.

⇧ **Eventually (though it make take weeks),** you should be able to ask the bird to come onto your hand. But set him back down after a few seconds.

What companion parrots need t

In order that your bird can spend as much time as possible out of the cage with you and your family, you'll need to teach him to accept a few simple requests or commands from you and other members of your household who wish to interact with him. Once trained to accept these requests, you will be able to ask your bird to fly to and from you or to leave certain places by using a verbal request. This allows you to have good control of your bird while he is out with you and means that he will be reasonably easy to supervise. In most cases, using reward-based training methods, a bird can be taught these requests in five to ten days. It is suggested you teach your bird the following requests in the order below.

STEP UP: This means step up onto my hand please. This is the first and perhaps most important request.

GO DOWN: This means please step off my hand onto another perch.

STAY: This means please do not come to me for the moment.

Assuming your bird can fly, make sure to teach these next requests as well:

GO: This means fly off me and go to another place (perhaps the stand or the cage).

ON HERE: This means please fly to me now.

OFF THERE: This means please leave your present perch/place and fly to another place, but do not fly to me.

Where should you train your bird?

In most cases, you can do the training in the room in which your bird is kept in. However, if the bird is aggressive around the cage, it may be easier to teach the first requests to step on and off your hand out of sight of the cage, perhaps in another room. In this case you'll need to have some way of getting your (untrained) bird to this room. In most cases, you can wheel the cage in to the other room, encourage the bird to leave the cage with a small food treat, then remove the cage before starting the training session. Nervous birds should always be taught

Training your Amazon

in the same room as their cage. It is best to arrange things so that the bird is asked to step up and down from places which are between waist and chest height, so the back of a chair is usually ideal. If this is the first time the bird is to be loose in the room, you should remove any objects or ornaments he may try to land on.

⇧ **Nervous birds should always** be trained in a familiar place, so train them in the same room as houses the cage.

An Amazon with ⇧ ⇨ **a fanned tail** and flashing eyes is overexcited. Take a break from training until he calms down.

⇦ **Make sure everything is ready** before starting to train your bird. With flying birds, remove any valuable ornaments which the bird might land on during a lesson.

The first requests: stepping up

Since you'll be using reward-based training, you first need to know how you are going to reward your bird's good behavior during these sessions. So, find something which you know your particular bird already really likes as this provides the essential motivation for him to work with you. The reward may be a favorite

⇧ *A few simple food-choice tests* will determine what your bird's really favorite items are.

food treat, or a particular toy, or having his head scratched. It's more effective to make sure that on training days the bird only gets these rewards by actually earning them: they should not be given for free, otherwise the bird has little incentive to cooperate. To determine a favorite food reward, offer your bird same-sized portions of a several items that he already likes all at once and see which he takes first.
Try a peanut, half a walnut, half a grape, and a sunflower seed. Many birds will do anything for even a small amount of peanut butter or margarine. Training sessions should be quite brief; two to four minutes is usually adequate.

Making the right preparations
Start by having your bird perched on the back of a chair and make sure he is calm but attentive. If the reward is a toy or food treat, you can show him this as you hold it in one hand. Say your bird's name and try to make eye contact, then approach him and place your other hand just above his feet and say "Step up." Your *step up* hand should be held with your four fingers in line but with your thumb out of the way. You can touch the bird just above his feet with this hand as you say "Step up." Repeat your request if necessary and make sure the bird can see the reward being offered. When he does step up, praise him enthusiastically, then after only a second or two, say "Go down" and encourage him to step down onto the chair back. Give him his reward straight away, with more verbal praise. Allow your bird plenty of time to appreciate the reward—it doesn't pay to hurry him at this stage. Repeat this once or twice more, then end the training session.

It's best just to have one training session on the first day and try to end this on a good note, even if the bird has only stepped up once and had his reward. On subsequent days you could have two or three sessions, but try to work with your bird when you know he is in a good, calm and receptive mood. *Whatever* the bird does during these sessions, make sure you always remain completely calm and appear confident. A calm atmosphere will greatly assist your bird in learning the requests. Soon, he should be stepping up and down more easily as he gets

and going down

STEPPING UP

⇧ **Step 1:** *Offer the bird your step-up hand while the reward is visible in your other hand and you clearly say* step up.

⇧ **Step 2:** *Keep your* step-up *hand completely still as the bird comes on to you; if you wobble or hesitate, the bird will be confused.*

⇧ **Step 3:** *Either give the reward now, or set the bird back down and then give it, but give him time to enjoy it.*

STEPPING DOWN

⇧ **Step 1:** *When asking the bird to step down, your hand should be a bit lower than the target perch he just stepped up from.*

⇧ **Step 2:** *Make the request to "Go down" and gently encourage the bird to step off you onto the perch on which he is to stand.*

⇧ **Step 3:** *Reward and praise your bird for all his efforts. Suitably rewarded birds learn new things very quickly.*

The *Stay* and *Go* requests

The *stay* request does not mean that a bird should stay exactly where it is since it is not appropriate to ask a bird to stay in one place for long periods. It is just used to ask a bird to refrain from approaching you for the moment, perhaps when you need to leave the room without the bird following you. If the bird approaches you and you do not wish him to step onto you or fly to you, hold your hand with the palm facing the bird and say "Stay." If the bird stops, praise and reward him. If he still tries to come to you, use your hand in this same gesture to block his approach, whether he is walking to you or flying to you. A flying bird will learn to turn around and land elsewhere. When he does, praise and reward him as usual. This *stay* request is very useful when other people are wary of interacting with a bird. If you have visitors who are not confident with birds, ask them to use this *stay* request as it will stop the bird from approaching them.

Teaching *go*

Go asks a bird to leave you by flying from you. Again, first make sure that you have a reward for your bird which you know he really likes and put this conspicuously on view at the place to which you will ask the bird to fly—perhaps on top of the cage or on his stand. Have the bird perched on your hand, 3 to 4ft (about 1m) away. Next, turn your hand at the wrist so the bird is facing *away from you and towards the intended landing place*. At the same time, use the index finger of your other hand, held lower down, to point to the place to which you want

the bird to fly. Make sure the bird has seen the reward and appears keen to want it. It can help to have someone else tempt the bird to fly by showing him the reward. Then, say "Go, go" and swing the hand with the bird on it gently but decisively in the direction you'd like him to go.

The bird should leave you and land on the intended perch/cage top. As soon as he does, *praise him as he takes his reward.* When he is happy to fly from this short distance, gradually increase the distance to the perch. Later, practice this request elsewhere until you can ask the bird to leave you wherever you happen to be. If after giving the *go* request, the bird flies off you but tries to return and land on you again, just use the *stay* request to prevent this.

⇧ **Step 1:** *Use your free hand to point to the perch; turn your other hand away and give the go request.*

⇑ **If the bird still decides** to come following a stay request, prevent him from landing on you with your stay hand held up in front of him.

⇑ **This is the gesture** to use to ask a bird to refrain from approaching you for the moment. Just have your palm facing the bird as you say "Stay."

⇑ **Step 2:** You can move your hand towards the perch and the bird should leave and fly to it.

⇑ **Step 3:** As he lands, praise him and leave him to enjoy his reward for a few minutes.

On here and *off there*

On here asks your bird to fly to you on a given cue. This is much easier if your bird is already flying to you spontaneously, but it can be taught after the above requests have been accepted. When your bird is already flying to you, start to associate this with a verbal cue by saying "On here" when he takes off and praise and reward him when he lands on you. If your bird does not come to you already, you need a powerful reward to ask him to do so, so make sure you have this first.

Place the bird on a familiar perch and stand about 3 to 4ft (1m) from him with your arm held out. Make sure that the bird can clearly see the reward you are offering. Your outstretched arm should be a little higher than the perch your bird is on, as birds prefer to fly up rather than

down when learning to come to you. Then say your bird's name and "On here" a few times. As the bird comes, stay completely still until he has landed and allow him plenty of time to enjoy his reward. If the bird does not come after a few attempts, avoid boredom setting in by taking a break and trying again later. Birds often fly towards you when you are leaving the room, so it can help to stand by the room door when teaching a bird to fly to you. Once your bird is flying from a short distance, gradually increase this at later sessions.

Off there

This is generally used as a safety request whereby you ask your bird to leave somewhere he should not have access to. So if a bird ever

ON HERE

⇧ **Step 1:** *For the first few sessions, only stand a few feet away, until the bird gains confidence in flying to you.*

⇧ **Step 2:** *Call the bird's name, show the reward prominently, and say "On here."*

lands on an unsafe place, such as an electrical appliance or perhaps a curtain rail, you can use this request to ask him to leave.

OFF THERE

Use a clear hand signal and say "Off there."

In practice you cannot teach this request predictably. However, when your bird does land somewhere that is unsafe or unsuitable, just approach him and say "Off there" as you wave one or both hands at him in an unfamiliar gesture. A wafting motion is often quite effective. You can also wave some harmless object, such as a handkerchief, near the bird. When he leaves, make sure that he does not try to land on you (give the *stay* request if needed) but lands on an appropriate perch, such as his stand or cage. Then praise him for his cooperation.

⇗ ⇧ **Birds should not be allowed** *to remain on any electrical apparatus, and the* off there *request is in this case essentially a safety measure. Be consistent about this request with your bird.*

⇧ **Step 3:** *Remain perfectly still as the bird comes in to land; this is very important when you begin.*

⇧ **Step 4:** *Give your reward immediately and praise the bird for his efforts at the same time.*

Further training hints

Generally, it should not be necessary to restrain a bird against his will, but occasionally you may have to do this. You may need to administer medication or take your bird to a vet or remove him quickly from some dangerous situation. Again, it is best to accustom the bird to what is needed in these situations before they arise.

Restraint must be done gently and calmly
There are two ways in to restrain a bird safely. The first involves asking the bird to *go down* on your chest. To do this, have the bird perched on your hand as usual, facing you and place your other hand over the bird's back as you say "Go down" and draw the bird to your chest while you withdraw the hand on which he was perched. The bird's feet will grip your clothing as he lets go of your hand. Praise the bird and reward him with a gentle head scratch using your free hand. You can then carry the bird in this way as you leave the area and put him down elsewhere, saying "Go down" as you do so. It's useful to practise this request by setting the bird down on various familiar places before using this method to return a bird to its cage. By this means, the bird won't associate it with having to go back to the cage and this will make such a request easier to use when you might need to put the bird in the cage without delay.

Careful use of a towel
The second method, involves the use of a towel, but this should not be confused with the practice of *forcibly* wrapping a bird up in a towel to tame

With the ⇨ *bird perched on you in the usual position, to cue the bird as to what you are about to do, say his name and keep eye contact.*

it. Such enforced towelling is not appropriate at all. However, it is useful to get your bird used to being held gently in a towel and this makes it easier for birds to be checked by a vet. Once the bird is trained in the requests as above, you can practice holding him in a towel, which should be a bland or neutral color, such as white or cream; birds are wary of dark or bold colors. To teach this, start by having the bird on your lap and offer him the corner of the towel to play with or to chew on. After a few sessions of this, let more of the towel come into contact with the bird's body. Eventually you should be able to accustom the bird to being held gently in the towel where you can restrain him for a few brief minutes. Reward the bird and encourage him at all times by giving praise, head scratches, or any reward he already likes.

⇧ **Draw the bird close** to your chest as you begin to cover his back with your free hand

⇧ **As the bird touches you,** lower the perch hand so he transfers his grip to your clothing.

⇧ **Once he is gripping** your clothing, praise the bird and give a gentle head scratch.

HOLDING A BIRD IN A TOWEL

⇧ **To help a bird** become used to towelling, initially allow him to chew a corner of it.

⇧ **Over time, the bird** should allow you to increase the amount of contact that you make with the towel.

⇧ **Reward the bird** when you can finally wrap him, but keep this first wrap very brief.

CHAPTER 9

Some frequently asked question:

This section looks at some frequently asked questions about parrot care.

Should I get another (second) bird?

This question is usually asked for two reasons. Either the first bird has bonded to one person only in the family and other family members would like a bird that can be their bird. Or the bird's main caregiver does not have the same amount of time to spend with the first bird as previously, and now considers getting another one as company for the first bird. The matter of a second bird should not be gone into lightly. There are many issues to consider before doing this. What sort of bird would you get, the same species or a different one? What age should your second bird be, an immature one or an adult? Will the second bird just pair up with your first bird? If it does, will it reject human companionship? Will it even become aggressive to you or others if it pairs up with the other bird?

Trying to predict the outcomes to these issues is very difficult, but some things are more predictable than others. When you have two adult birds of the same species and opposite sex, they are very likely to pair up. This means they may prefer one another's company to yours. One or both of them may become aggressive to people if they perceive humans are interfering with their relationship with each other. If a second bird is not closely related to the first, this is less likely to happen. Here the birds may become friendly towards each other without pairing up fully and this result is ideal.

However, these are not predictable outcomes. So if you do decide to get a second bird and want to ensure both birds appreciate human company as companion animals, you might be best getting a species which is not closely related to your first bird. Other species which originate from South America, such as another Amazon or a conure, could be tried with your bird. To further reduce the chances of birds pairing up exclusively with each other, they should each be housed in their own large cage but with both cages situated in the same room.

If your second bird is ⇨ of the same species and of opposite sex, there is every chance they will pair up and one or both birds may then reject you.

⇧ **Other species which originate** from South America, like this conure, tend to have more behaviors in common with Amazons.

◁ **Introducing a new bird** needs to be done with care. Initial reactions can be very misleading! So you need to repeat these sessions several times.

◁ **The blue-fronted Amazon** on the right shows a keen, friendly interest in this orange-winged Amazon, but she is more wary.

Talking and use of a harness

When will my bird start to talk?

Most Amazon parrots learn to talk quite well, usually by the time they are two years old, but some species are more inclined to talk than others. The blue-fronted, double yellow-headed, and yellow-naped Amazons are well known for their talking abilities. However, talking cannot be guaranteed and some Amazons never talk. Unlike grey parrots, Amazons, being more extroverted, will often talk more freely, even in the company of strangers. Lone birds are more likely to reproduce human speech, since they have no other birds to share their natural calls with. The value of talking will depend on the method you use to teach speech. While Amazons are good mimics, as they are very intelligent birds they can also be taught to use human speech in its proper context, much like a very young child. With this in mind, it is more rewarding and useful if, when giving a bird something such as a toy or a food treat, you state the name of the object clearly to the bird. The bird may learn to associate the object with its name and then ask for it by naming it. This use of talking will be of more value than mere mimicry.

Blue-fronted Amazons are well known for their talking abilities.

⇩ **By associating an object,** such as this toy ball, with its actual name, some Amazons can be taught to use many words in their proper context.

The bird will be more motivated to use speech with objects it already desires.

Can I use a harness so that I can safely take my bird outdoors?

No type of leg restraint can be used on a parrot, as this can cause the leg to be dislocated if it were to try to take flight. Although most Amazons dislike anything touching their feathers, some will accept a harness which can be used, with care, to take your bird outdoors. The harness is fitted around the bird's body and has a strap below for you to hold on to. There are several different types of harnesses. The better ones have no metal parts on them and feature an elasticated leash which ensures the bird is not jolted suddenly if it does fly off you. Birds will need to be properly trained, with care, if they are to accept a harness,

◁ *This harness has no metal parts and the leash is elasticated.*

and this should be done at a pace that the bird finds comfortable. On the first few occasions, make sure the bird wears the harness for a *few seconds only* and do this in a familiar indoor location. If the bird seems comfortable with this, gradually increase the time that the bird wears the harness at each session. If at any stage the bird does not seem comfortable with the harness, *do not persist with forcing this on a bird*. Instead, consider building a day-flight/aviary.

⇩ *Some birds may take to a harness but most birds object to the feel of the straps on their bodies.*

Wing clipping

Should my bird have its wings clipped?

There are various types of wing clipping; some methods are more severe than others. Clipping involves shortening some or all of the bird's main flight feathers—the primary feathers which are the ten outermost wing feathers. This is sometimes done to one wing only in order deliberately to unbalance the bird if it attempts to fly; this is the most dangerous type of clip. Other forms of clipping involve clipping both wings evenly but lightly with some of the primaries left intact. These methods are less crude and allow the bird at least to fly down and land safely indoors. Although the molting process should eventually see a regrowth of any clipped feathers, this process can be problematic for clipped birds. Where the delicate new blood feathers have to grow down without the protection of neighbouring feathers they are liable to be broken and may bleed profusely. This can also be painful for the bird.

The commonest reasons giving for clipping are to control the bird's movements or for safety. However, all birds, whether clipped or not, are subject to some risks; clipped birds are just at risk in different circumstances. If clipped birds escape, there is more chance of them being caught by a dog or cat or being run over by a vehicle. Since clipping prevents upward flight, such birds are also vulnerable to becoming very fearful or phobic and can have greatly reduced confidence. Parrots have no behavioral response to cope with being unable to fly and many find flightlessness very distressing. A bird's most important and instinctive means of escaping from any fearful situation is simply to fly away, preferably to a higher perch. Clipping denies the bird this most vital escape mechanism.

The training section in this book explains how you can teach your bird some simple requests or commands to control its flight. This usually only takes a few days, and these requests, once taught, give you all the control you need, and your bird can behave more naturally by being able to fly. It is the provision of opportunities for

⇩ *A typical 'normal' wing clip which is still inflicted on many birds. If this bird were clipped as shown, it would lose most of its braking power.*

Clipped birds can still be frightened and try to fly away, but the consequences can be painful crash landings.

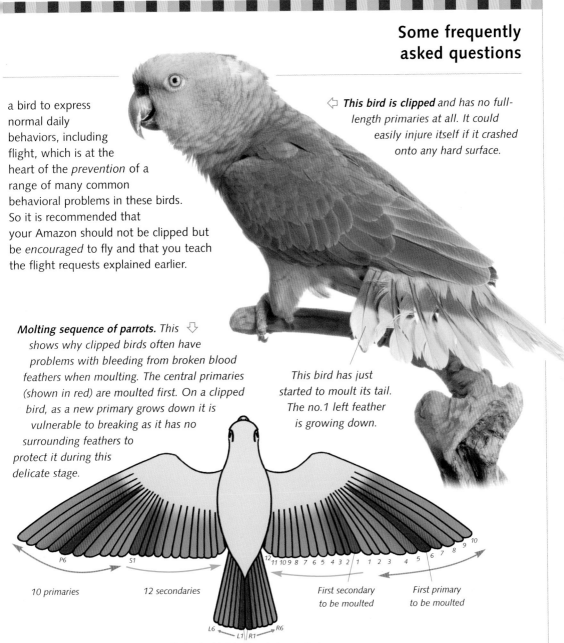

a bird to express normal daily behaviors, including flight, which is at the heart of the *prevention* of a range of many common behavioral problems in these birds. So it is recommended that your Amazon should not be clipped but be *encouraged* to fly and that you teach the flight requests explained earlier.

◁ **This bird is clipped** and has no full-length primaries at all. It could easily injure itself if it crashed onto any hard surface.

Molting sequence of parrots. This ⇩ shows why clipped birds often have problems with bleeding from broken blood feathers when moulting. The central primaries (shown in red) are moulted first. On a clipped bird, as a new primary grows down it is vulnerable to breaking as it has no surrounding feathers to protect it during this delicate stage.

This bird has just started to moult its tail. The no.1 left feather is growing down.

P6   S1   12 11 10 9 8 7 6 5 4 3 2 1 | 1 2 3 4 5 6 7 8 9 10

10 primaries   12 secondaries   First secondary to be moulted   First primary to be moulted

L6 ← L1 | R1 → R6

First pair of tail feathers to be moulted

Keeping an unclipped bird safe

What precautions should I observe if my bird's wings are not clipped?

When keeping birds that have not been wing-clipped it is important to follow some common-sense precautions.

Your bird should be properly supervised at all times when out of its cage and should be taught the flight requests explained on pages 62-5

Be aware of common household dangers. Birds should not be in rooms which have ceiling fans, open external doors and windows, or large mirrors. Large-pane windows can be very confusing for a bird, so these should have blinds or curtains hung in front of them. Do not allow your bird into the kitchen as there are too many dangers here for birds including sources of heat and potentially toxic fumes from Teflon-coated pans.

Ensure that your Amazon has several places outside the cage which it can use as perches. You may find it easier to manage the bird if these places are no higher than your head – for example, the backs of chairs and sofas, window ledges, and tables. In any new situation, Amazons should not just be left to get on with things on their own. As highly social creatures, Amazons need guidance and encouragement from you.

So, when introducing a bird to any new place or new room, make sure to show the bird the places you would like him to use as perches. Just ask him to "Go down" onto these places using

the *go down* request you have already taught him and reward him on the first few occasions with a tidbit or a favourite small toy to play with. When the bird is used to these places, he will be more confident about knowing where he can land when he does fly. Later, try using the *go* command to ask the bird to fly to these places from your hand.

While it is acceptable for a flying bird to *land* on your shoulder, the shoulder should not be seen as a normal perch. Always transfer the bird from your shoulder to your hand as soon as he lands there; just use the *step up* command for this. Your *hand* should be the bird's normal perch when it is on you, not your arm or your shoulder.

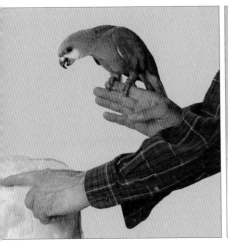

⇧ **By making sure you introduce** a bird to a room properly, the bird will fly with confidence and tend to land on those places you have already introduced it to as suitable perches.

⇦ **Common-sense precautions** will keep your bird safe. Large windows should be partially obscured with curtains. If you allow a bird to stay on your shoulder, you risk forgetting that it is there. Many birds fly off as their caregivers accidentally walk outside with the bird still on their shoulder.

Health and hygiene

Can I toilet train my bird?

While Amazons can be taught to use certain places to pass their droppings, this needs to be done with care. You will soon notice from your bird's body language when he is about to pass droppings. At this point, you can try moving him to one of the places you would like him to use, then praise the bird just after he has passed his droppings. However, it is important to have *several places* which your bird can use, otherwise he may become conditioned to only going to one place and this can cause him problems. Eventually, your bird will associate these certain

⇧ **Droppings can be cleaned up** easily with a tissue and a suitable cleaning product.

places as suitable and will make his own way there without your help to pass his droppings. Alternatively, you can lay some paper beneath the places the bird uses as perches to catch the droppings or just clean up immediately using a tissue and a good household cleaning product.

How often should the cage be cleaned?

It's best to use old newspapers for covering the cage floor and these should be changed every day. Once a week the whole cage, including the perches, should be scrubbed clean using a mild, diluted disinfectant and hot water. Some bird supplement suppliers sell bird-safe disinfectant although other disinfectants are usually safe when diluted. Follow the manufacturer's recommendations regarding the strength of the solution it is advisable to use. Where a roosting box is used, birds rarely soil this, but the box should be cleaned thoroughly like the cage, once a week. The wood shavings or newspaper lining the box should be replaced once a week.

How often should food bowls be cleaned?

These should be washed thoroughly at least once every day in hot water and mild detergent, and then rinsed in plain cold water before refilling with food and water. Again bird supplement suppliers sell bird-safe antiseptic which you may wish to use as well when washing the food bowls each day.

What about general health and hygiene? With a common-sense approach, healthy birds pose few health problems for most people. However, care should be taken to avoid bird's droppings contaminating anywhere where human food might be prepared; so it's best to prevent birds having access to these areas, particularly in households with young children or elderly people, whose immune systems may not be as strong as other people's. In rare cases a disease called psittacosis may be transmitted to humans through inhalation of dust contaminated with infected particles in droppings. If you are ever ill and need to visit your doctor, always state that you keep birds in case this is relevant. If you think your bird is actually passing psittacosis in its droppings then the bird needs to be seen by a vet immediately for treatment. Fortunately psittacosis is rarely seen in humans but a far more common problem is people's allergy to feather dust.

Remember to wash your hands before preparing your bird's food. Birds are sensitive to many common household chemicals so make sure your hands are clean and uncontaminated before handling any food or the bird.

⇩ **Cage bars will need to be cleaned** once a week using diluted disinfectant and warm water.

◁ **Newspaper remains the best** floor covering for your bird's cage, and this should be changed each day.

⇧ **Perches can get very dirty** with food waste, so scrub these clean at least weekly.

Beak and claw care

Do I need to trim my bird's claws.

Parrots need fairly sharp claws to grip smooth perches properly. When a bird has blunt claws, it may slip off some perches or even fall and crash. So, in most cases, it is not necessary to trim a bird's claws regularly, they will only need checking occasionally and trimming if really overgrown. A wild bird's claws wear down naturally and are kept at the right length. In captivity, some excessive growth may occur and cause the bird problems. Rather than using

These claws are clearly overgrown and need trimming.

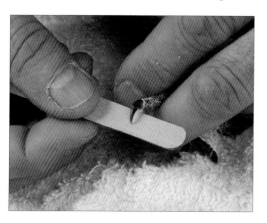

With long claws filed down, this bird perches more comfortably.

⇧ **By filing any excess growth off**, *rather than using clippers, there is no risk of accidentally cutting through a blood vessel in the bird's claws.*

⇧ **An abrasive perch like this** *can be screwed to the bars of the cage; it should not be a top perch.*

clippers for this, it is best to use a small file or fine abrasive material to simply file off any excess growth. You'll need a helper to hold the bird carefully in a towel. Alternatively, you can use an abrasive perch in the cage. However, parrots should not be required to use an abrasive perch for long periods as this can cause some discomfort. So the perch should not be a favourite or top perch, but one lower down in the cage, perhaps beside a food or water bowl.

Do I need to trim my bird's beak?

The beak is extremely sensitive and it is not recommended you ever try to trim your bird's beak. If it is overgrown and actually causing the bird problems in eating, take the bird to an experienced avian vet for advice on this matter.

The upper beak is naturally long and sharp on most parrots.

Should I let a bird take food from my mouth?

It is recommended that you do not allow your bird to take food from your mouth. Our mouths and the mouths of birds both contain many different types of bacteria and you should not put yourself or your bird at risk of contaminating one another in this way. Many people have their lips bitten when doing this, and this can require a visit to hospital.

What should I do when I go on vacation?

If you have recently acquired a young bird, the bird will be very dependent on you, so you should simply not go away at all until the bird is more than a year old. To a very young bird, the sudden departure of the person to whom it is bonded can be extremely stressful. Under such circumstances, the bird may start to pluck out its own feathers. In the wild, an Amazon's parents would never desert the young bird and immature birds have no behavioral adaptation to cope with such a loss. With older birds, it is best to ensure they are used to the person who is going to care for them while you are away. The bird sitter should be familiar with the bird's needs and be able to handle the bird in a similar way to you. Provided the bird sitter allows the bird out of the cage for several hours each day and the bird relates at least reasonably well to him or her, and that other aspects of its care (such as food and caging) remain the same, the bird should cope well with your temporary absence. Some small animal boarding places do take parrots in as well, but you may feel more confident knowing your bird is with someone you already know and trust.

⬆ ***Get your bird used*** *to going in and out of a travelling cage before you actually need to use it.*

CHAPTER 10

Maturing birds and biting

Growing up: from baby to adult

It isn't helpful to project human emotions and values onto parrots and parrots should never be blamed for anything they do. *All* the behaviors your bird displays are done because the bird is either trying to obtain something it needs or trying to avoid something it dislikes. Parrots do not try to annoy anyone. Whether any behavior is reinforced (is likely to be repeated) often depends on how we respond to such behaviors. As a young Amazon begins to mature at two to three years old, the changes in its behavior are much the same as you would expect to see in any other animal, such as a puppy or a kitten growing up. The "cuddly tame" baby bird on sale at a breeder's premises or a pet shop has a very different set of urges when it becomes an adult. This is quite normal. The bird may appear to 'test you' from time to time with some of its behaviors, but by ensuring that your bird accepts the requests described in the training section, you should not have any serious problems as he matures.

Biting

Most parrot people do get bitten from time to time and usually this is only a minor problem. However, *hard* biting which causes pain needs to be addressed carefully, otherwise you may unintentionally reinforce such biting and make matters worse. Biting often first occurs as birds begin to mature and the first incidents are commonly caused by the bird simply getting overexcited, perhaps while in a playful mood. So always interact with your bird in ways that do not result in such overexcitement. If you are bitten hard, do *not* return the bird to its cage, otherwise you will soon have difficulty in doing even that! And do not even think of reprimanding the bird, as that will certainly reinforce further biting behavior.

The most effective response is to simply turn your back on the bird, walk out of the room, and close the door behind you, leaving the bird on its own for two or three minutes. When you return, wait for the bird to interact with you, then carry on as normal. If biting occurs again, remain calm and simply repeat this move by leaving the bird alone for a few minutes. In most cases the bird soon makes the connection between biting and being left on its own and then it has an incentive to cease biting.

⇧ **These part-parent-reared** blue-fronted Amazons are very endearing birds at 11 weeks old. However, their submissive behavior relates to their needs as babies. Within two to three years they will become much more confident and assertive.

⇩ **With its tail fanned** and eyes pinning, this bird is very hyped up! So back off for now.

⇦ **If a person's hand movements** are too quick, or the bird becomes overexcited, the risk of biting increases. Prevention is far better than cure; so move slowly but confidently when training or re-training your bird.

Preventing self-plucking

Amazon parrots can be prone to self-plucking and this problem is associated with captivity; wild parrots do not self-pluck. Any self-plucking bird should be examined by a specialist avian vet to check its medical condition and diet. There is increasing evidence that self-plucking arises from behavioral frustrations where a bird is not able to carry out its normal daily behaviors. Also, the habit may be unintentionally reinforced in the bird when caregivers say "No" or gives the bird some attention during plucking. It is best to *say* nothing to the bird but leave the room each time the bird self-plucks. Assuming the bird likes you, this gives him an incentive to cease plucking, at least while in your company. Amazons most vulnerable to self-plucking are those whose conditions include the factors described below.

They are solitary 'pet' birds who have been hand-reared; they spend long periods during the day in their cages rather than out interacting with their people or other birds; they also have little or no opportunities to fly and no opportunities to forage for hidden foods.

Foraging opportunities

Wild Amazons spend much time searching for food and they have a strong behavioral need to carry out foraging behaviors. But pet parrots, with a food bowl a few inches from them at all times are very prone to severe boredom. The frustration of being unable to perform foraging behaviors can cause many behavioral problems. To prevent and help cure self-plucking, the bird should have a range of toys which he actually plays with, including puzzle toys in which food can be hidden. These can be bought but you can also make your own at little or no cost. Try hiding some seeds in a cardboard tube filled with newspaper, or a tidbit inside a small box filled with crumpled paper. Food hung up in small baskets or in bird-feeders used for wild birds can also be used.

Giving your bird opportunities to fly, both indoors and in an outdoor aviary will also help. Provide plenty of items that your bird can simply chew up to destruction. Use short lengths of cotton or hemp ropes, fresh branches from any fruit or nut trees, strips of rawhide leather, or even old phone books to chew up. The key thing is to keep your bird's beak and brain busy. With plenty of out-of-cage time and lots of things to chew up, your bird is much less likely to chew on his own feathers.

◁ *When self-plucking occurs,* it responds best if treatment starts as soon as possible. While it can occur at almost any age, it manifests itself most often in hand-reared birds as they begin to mature at around two to four years old.

Common behavioral problems

Busy birds are less likely to self-pluck.

Amazons need to be stimulated if behavioral problems are to be prevented.

◁ **There are many puzzle toys** made for parrots. These require the bird to work out how to extract foods from them. Having a range of these toys available for your bird will help to keep him busy.

This orange-winged Amazon ⇨ is given pine-cones laced with some favourite food treat such as peanut butter to encourage foraging and food-processing activities.

Many Amazons ⇨ **like tearing up** destructible toys, as this replicates wild foraging behaviours.

Nervous and phobic parrots

Amazons which cannot fly, perhaps through being wing-clipped, are susceptible to becoming phobic and showing an exaggerated fear of seemingly harmless actions, objects or people. When an Amazon is nervous or fearful he usually remains silent and holds his body feathers down tightly. If the cause of the problem is not removed promptly, the bird may start to panic wildly. Sometimes the fear is so great the bird may thrash around in its cage. This behavior has nothing to do with aggression—it means the bird is really terrified of something. You should remove the source of your bird's fear *immediately*, even if the source is you! Just walk away, even leave the room, but do so immediately. Make sure your bird has a perch in the cage which is above your eye level. This helps to reduce the bird's fear of people who come close. Birds do not show any evidence of being able to accept reassurance as we humans do, so if the bird is afraid of you or something you have done, attempts at reassurance are not only pointless but can make a bad situation much worse.

Don't rush in to help a bird

For example, if your bird crash-lands somewhere and you approach him immediately to reassure him, it is very likely he will associate you with any pain or fear he may be feeling at this point, and begin to fear you as part of the cause of his pain. In this situation, it is wiser to remove yourself from the bird for a few moments until he has collected his senses and calmed down. Only then make yourself available to him, but even then, ask him to come to you, rather than approaching him closely.

Getting a bird to overcome its nervousness may take some time and has to be done at a pace which is comfortable for the bird. See the section on nervous birds on pages 56-7 and follow the guidelines there. You'll need to be patient, working slowly and carefully with the bird, using whatever rewards you know the bird is likely to accept. If other people can work with the bird better than you, then give them the opportunity to do so at first. You can then help later when the bird's confidence is showing some signs of returning.

⇧ **Wing-clipped Amazons** sometimes lack confidence and become very nervous birds.

⇧ **If a bird has become fearful** of its main caregiver, the process of retaming and retraining the bird may take some time. It is vital that you always work at a pace which is comfortable and not stressful for the bird.

⇦ **If a bird crash-lands,** perhaps because something has startled him, wait a few moments before thinking of approaching him. You must not associate yourself with any discomfort or fear the bird may be feeling.

Destructive chewing and nois

As wild birds, Amazons spend much time chewing on wood, leaves and buds in the treetops; this is part of their natural foraging behavior. While pet birds have food available at all times, they still have a strong natural urge to carry out these foraging and chewing behaviors. If birds have no access to suitable things on which to chew, they are very likely to chew anything they can get their beaks into, such as items of furniture, doors and any vulnerable ornaments.

⇧ **You can easily make** suitable foraging toys. First sprinkle a few seeds or nuts on a piece of newspaper.

⇧ **If you don't provide** your bird with suitable chewing items, he might find his own alternatives!

Make some chew toys for your bird

It is important to provide your bird with destructible toys to keep him busy. While you can certainly buy these from pet shops and mail-order firms, you can also make your own. Try using wooden clothespins (remove the spring), pieces of hardwood (such as oak, apple, cherry, hazel, etc.), cardboard, newspaper, pine cones, rawhide leather strips, or short lengths of cord

made from natural fibres such as cotton, hemp, or jute. Also, providing your bird with opportunities to forage for some of his favorite foods hidden in puzzle toys will help to divert him from chewing unsuitable objects. Again you can buy these toys from pet product suppliers or devise your own versions. Amazons will soon learn to search out food treats hidden in pieces of crumpled newspaper inserted into cardboard tubes or small cardboard boxes.

Noise

Amazons are usually quite noisy birds and it is part of their normal behavior as adults to have regular screaming sessions in the morning and late afternoon. These usually last no more than half an hour. If the bird does start to make a

⇧ **Then fold it** and fit it inside a cardboard tube.

⇧ **Make sure the bird** sees you doing this, then offer it to him.

⇧ **Amazons often become** quite enthusiastic about these home-made chew toys.

loud repetitive noise for much of the day, then this is likely to be due to boredom. Birds which spend too long in their cages will be prone to this behavior, so they need to be out more and be kept occupied. In cases where a bird has plenty of time out of the cage but still starts to make a loud noise which causes a problem, it is vital that you do not inadvertently reward this behavior by giving the bird any attention, including saying "No" to him. The best action is for *everyone* simply to leave the room each time your bird starts to produce the unwanted noise, or when you feel it has lasted for too long. Eventually most birds realize that their behavior has caused you to leave. When your parrot makes this connection, he will have the incentive to stop making the unwanted noise.

You should expect some noise from Amazons, but try ⇨ *just leaving the room if the noise becomes unacceptable.*

CHAPTER 11

First aid and general health care

Providing your bird has a good diet, plenty of time each day out of the cage during which he can fly, and a stimulating environment with a good relationship with his human family, he should stay physically and mentally healthy. However, you should be prepared for the possibility of illness long before it occurs by having made contact with a good specialist bird vet. It is important to use a vet who has considerable experience of treating birds, rather than an ordinary vet whose skills may not include avian medicine. It is also recommended that your bird should be examined at least once a year for a general health checkup. Most bird vets are members of the Association of Avian Vets and various websites list their contact details. Bird vets are also listed in avian publications each month. Good bird vets will have some or all of the following facilities:

- Anaesthesia by isofluorane gas (this is a very safe method of anaesthesia for birds).
- Ability to do imping (restoring flight by repairing a bird's wings following any wing-clipping).
- Ability to do complete blood count and biochemistry tests.
- Use of an endoscope for internal examinations.
- Ability to take tissue samples (biopsies) for testing.
- Staff who know how to handle parrots correctly, using a towel (not gloves) to minimise stress.
- 24-hour hospitalisation facilities for birds.

Recognising ill health in your bird

Healthy birds generally remain active for most, but not all, of the day. They have bright, wide open eyes and clean nostrils (no discharge). Breathing is silent. Healthy birds are alert and will take an interest in the world around them. The body feathers will be relaxed and slightly smoothed down; neither puffed up nor held down with an excessive tightness. The bird should be eating normally and passing droppings normally, without undue straining. The area around the vent

The vent of the bird should be clear of droppings.

underneath the tail should not be soiled by the bird's droppings. When resting or sleeping, a healthy bird usually stands on one foot for much of the time. If your bird does not show these normal healthy signs, something may be wrong. Remember, sick birds will always try to *hide signs of illness,* so by the time a bird appears unwell, it is usually very ill indeed. Make sure to act without any delay in getting your bird treated if you ever think he may be unwell.

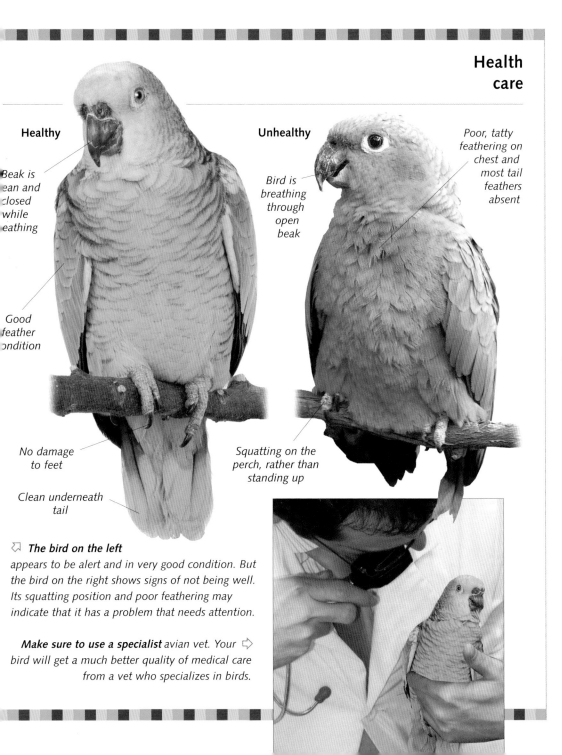

Healthy

Unhealthy

Beak is clean and closed while breathing

Bird is breathing through open beak

Poor, tatty feathering on chest and most tail feathers absent

Good feather condition

No damage to feet

Squatting on the perch, rather than standing up

Clean underneath tail

↖ **The bird on the left**
appears to be alert and in very good condition. But the bird on the right shows signs of not being well. Its squatting position and poor feathering may indicate that it has a problem that needs attention.

Make sure to use a specialist avian vet. Your ⇨
bird will get a much better quality of medical care from a vet who specializes in birds.

Recognizing sick birds

Sick birds often appear tired with fluffed up feathers and sunken, dull or half-closed eyes. They may have difficulty balancing or using a perch and may go to the floor of the cage instead. Sick birds often shows signs of being less aware of things going on around them. The droppings may not be normal and the bird may not be eating as usual. Sick birds often lose weight and this change can be rapid. Make sure you know your bird's normal weight and check this from time to time.

⇧ *Some good quality kitchen scales* can be used to check for any variations in your bird's weight.

Sick birds: what to do
If the bird can be weighed without causing further stress, then do so and write this measurement down. Sick birds usually gain great benefit from simply being put somewhere very warm—79 to 86°F (26 to 30°C)—and kept out of bright light. You can supply heat using a ceramic infrared heat lamp placed above the cage (this emits heat without any light). Position

this so that the bird can move away from the lamp if at any time it feels too hot. Use a thermometer to check the temperature around the cage (but keep this out of reach of the bird). The provision of heat will mean the bird will need to drink regularly, so make sure that the bird has easy access to drinking water and wet foods such as grapes or apples. Once the bird is receiving heat treatment, phone your vet, explain the bird's symptoms, and get emergency advice without delay. When taking your bird to the vet, keep it very warm all the time. Stress alone can make things worse for the bird, so always act calmly. Restrict the bird's ability to see out of its carrier cage during traveling as this also helps to reduce stress.

Items for your bird's First Aid needs:
- Avian vet's contact details.
- Cotton balls and cotton swabs—used to help stop bleeding.
- Styptic pencil (to stop bleeding of claws or damaged beak only).
- Antibiotic ointment for treatment of wounds.
- Avian antiseptic.

⇩ **This Amazon has access** to additional heat from an infra-red heat lamp if it wants to be warmer.

⇧ **If your bird is not tame,** you may need to hold him in a towel to transfer him to a travel cage.

⇧ **A dark cage** with restricted viewing will keep the bird more calm than an all-wire or see-through type will do.

- Electrolyte solution, e.g. Prolyte-C from Aviform, UK—helps birds to recover after treatment.
- Avian multivitamin powder
- Glucose powder—this is dissolved in water as an emergency food for birds having difficulty eating.
- Towel—this should be a bland color, such as white or cream. Dark towels may frighten the bird.
- Ceramic infrared heat lamp, or hospital cage.
- Thermometer.
- Small syringes and a bent spoon for giving medicine or food.
- Forceps.
- Pair of small sharp scissors.
- Hand-feeding formula; in case you need to force-feed the bird.
- Traveling cage with one low-level securely fitted perch.
- Good quality electric scales.

CHAPTER 12

Recovering a lost bird

Most parrots escape through an open door or window, or, with shoulder birds, fly off their keeper if they accidentally walk outside with the bird *(right)*. So, never allow a parrot to stay on your shoulder!

In the event of an escape, what should you do? First, you should have these items to hand:

- A good pair of binoculars.
- Some of your bird's favorite food treats and the food bowl from his cage.
- A traveling case and/or cloth holding bag with drawstrings to put the bird in if you do catch him

If the bird panics while escaping, it will fly a great distance before eventually landing exhausted, in a tree. If the bird has not panicked, it will not usually go so far. Most parrots find the outdoors a very confusing place simply because it is unfamiliar, but their instincts tell them to stay high up, usually in a tree, often the tallest tree in the area. The bird may then climb down and hide within the foliage. In winter, you may find the bird by direct searching, using your binoculars, but in summer it can be extremely difficult to spot a parrot in a leafy tree. So, it's best to call your bird's name and listen for his replies.

Also make copies of a short note with a good photograph and description of your bird and details of when it was lost and your contact details. Post this to as many people as you can in your neighbourhood. Finders of strange birds often tell the police, local radio stations, vets, and the ASPCA, so make sure you also inform them of your escaped bird.

Coaxing your bird down

When you find your bird, he will be unlikely to fly down to you, so you should try to devise a way he can walk towards you through the branches. It helps if you have a ladder and climb up towards the bird and tempt him towards you with a food treat. When the bird is near you he will still obey the *step up* request so you should secure him once he's on your hand. You should have a bag or box ready (out of sight of the bird) into which you can put him before you climb down. You can make a suitable bag from a small pillowcase. This should have a drawstring and a strap which goes over your shoulder to leave your hands free when coming down the ladder. Alternatively you can lower the bag down to the ground on a long line.

If you do not recover the bird but know where he is, return before light the next morning as he is still very likely to be there and try again. In summer, this will mean getting there before 4am.

⇧ **Escaped birds often land** in the tallest tree in the
area and are nervous about coming lower down.

⇩ **A bag with drawstrings** can be used to
contain the bird once secured.

Binoculars are vital, ⇨
though foliage
may limit their
usefulness
in summer.

Index

Note: Page numbers set in *italic* type refer to captions to pictures; page numbers set in **bold** type indicate the main subject reference.

Picture Credits

Published by
Interpet Publishing,
Vincent Lane,
Dorking,
Surrey RH4 3YX,
England

© 2007 **Interpet Publishing Ltd.**
All rights reserved

ISBN 978 1 84286 171 4

Editor: **Philip de Ste. Croix**
Designer: **Philip Clucas MCDS**
Photographer: **Neil Sutherland**
Diagram artwork: **Martin Reed**
Index: **Amanda O'Neill**
Production management: **Consortium, Suffolk**
Print production: **Sino Publishing House Ltd, Hong Kong**

Unless otherwise credited below, all the photographs that appear in this book were taken by **Neil Sutherland** especially for Interpet Publishing. The publisher would also like to thank Mike Taylor at **Northern Parrots** (www.24Parrot.com) for kindly supplying the picture of the parrot stand that is credited below, and **Anton van der Ploeg** who supplied a selection of pictures of young Amazons.

Frank Lane Picture Agency/flpa-images.co.uk: 10 top right (David Hosking), 11 centre right (Jurgen and Christine Sohns), 11 bottom left (Pete Oxford/Minden Pictures), 12 (Jurgen and Christine Sohns), 13 bottom right (Claus Meyer/Minden Pictures), 15 top (Tui De Roy/Minden Pictures), 23 top right (Jurgen and Christine Sohns).

Greg Glendell: 81 top, 93 top.

iStockphoto.com:
AM29: 8 bottom right.
Griselda Amorim: 22.
Jean-Yves Benedeyt: 48.
James Benet: 27 top.
Chai kian shin: 45 centre right.
Julie de Leseleuc: 82, 83 top right.
Brian Doty: 10 top left.
Lee Feldstein: 6, 20, 21 bottom right.

Olga Gabay: 17 top right.
Iztok Grilc: 93 bottom right.
Dawn Jagroop: 13 top inset.
Elena Kalistratova: 27 bottom centre.
Paul Piebinga: 84 top left.
Michael Puerzer: 3 inset bottom left, 15 bottom.
Ray Roper: 9 bottom left.
McKevin Shaughnessy: 27 bottom right.

Northern Parrots: 49 bottom left.

Shutterstock Inc.:
Stephen Coburn: 89 top right.
Steve Cukrov: 10 bottom left, 23 top left.
Joseph Gareri: 9 top left.
Wendy Kaveney Photography: 89 bottom right.
Andrew Kua Seng How: 69 right.
Eric Isselée: 3 inset right, 72, 73 top.
Diana Mary Jorgenson: 85 top left.
Jill Lang: 24 top left, 25 top.
B. Speckart: 13 top.
Mark E. Stout: 69 left.
Tim Zurowski: 26.

Anton van der Ploeg: 17 top left, 21 top left, 21 top right, 21 bottom left.